The artistic value of Master Frans Bleiji is immense. His colours, his shapes, his drawing describe the world with lots of details and skill. His dialectics surpasses the boundaries of true realism and narrates the personal re-elaboration of memories, of everyday life, of old-times toys. The light of his works remembers his land, the Netherlands, it's a light soft light borrowed from the Northern fogs. It's a diffused and not overpowering light that is full of a strong sensitivity that knocks softly at the door of the soul but does not ring the bell. An unbeatable painting in technique, reminds us Rembrandt and Vermeer for its tones but which describes our contemporaneity. Bleiji has within himself the Dutch artistic past and dominates and uses the modern to excite, to enchant and to make thinking the viewer spectator. Objects thus acquire a voice, they become the spokesman for a fantastic world that becomes real. With Bleiji it's easy to forget the existence of the border between reality and fantasy, and everyone becomes part of a world of timeless dreams.

Il valore artistico del Maestro Frans Bleiji è immenso. I suoi colori, le sue forme, il suo tratto descrivono il mondo con dovizia di particolari e abilità. La sua dialettica supera i confini del realismo fine a sé stesso e narra le rielaborazioni personali di ricordi, della quotidianità, dei giocattoli di un tempo. La luce delle sue opere ricorda la sua terra, l'Olanda, una luce morbida leggera mutuata dalle brume del Nord. Una luce diffusa e non prepotente, che è pieno supporto di una sensibilità spiccata che bussa dolcemente alla porta dell'animo ma non suona il campanello. Una pittura imbattibile nella tecnica, che ci ricorda Rembrandt e Vermeer per i toni e che descrive però la nostra contemporaneità. Bleiji ha dentro di se il passato artistico dell'Olanda e lo domina e usa il moderno per emozionare, incantare e far riflettere lo spettatore. Gli oggetti così acquistano una voce propria, diventano i portavoce di un mondo fantastico che diventa reale. Con Bleiji facile è il dimenticare l'esistenza del confine tra realtà e fantasia e ognuno diventa partecipe di un mondo raffinati sogni senza tempo.

Dino Marasà

Frans Bleiji
Burg. Knappertlaan 218b - 3117 JA Schiedam (Netherland)
Website; www.fransbleiji.nl - Email; info@fransbleiji.nl

On cover: Still life with wooden spoon, oil on panel, 42x33 cm

Frans Bleiji was born in November 6th 1950 in Leiden. He made his first steps in art in 1984 at the Volksuniversity in Vlaardingen, his teacher noticed the progress he made in a short time and he gave him the advice to start a education at the Academy. So he went in 1986 at the Royal Academy of Art in The Hague. In the second year he stopped it because the lessons became to abstract and such they won't fit to his way of working, so he became a self-thought artist. A note about his work (trompe-l'oeil). He has objects stuck on or pinned to the canvas. It certainly seems like it; you bend over and involuntary to feel with your fingers whether the push pin has or hasn't actually been inserted into the canvas. It hasn't. One of many notables reactions to Frans Bleiji's work, referring to the use of trompe-l' oeil. By using the techniques of chiaroscuro and especially trompe-l'oeil, Frans succeeds in breathtakingly capturing the essence of the subject and the underlying thoughts. But he is not an artist who likes to tie himself down to one particular way of working although his approach should always contain a aspect of realism. Whatever course he chooses to pursue, realism will always be part of the new route. Frans is always searching for the third dimension on the flat surface, so it was given to him the nickname "the shadow artist" in a newspaper article. His works are in private collections in: Netherland, Belgium, France, England, America, Ireland, Curaçao and Switzerland.

Frans Bleiji è nato il 6 novembre 1950 a Leiden. Ha compiuto i suoi primi passi nell'arte nel 1984 alla Volksuniversity di Vlaardingen dove gli fu consigliato dal docente di iniziare a studiare all'Accademia Reale di Belle Arti dell'Aia che iniziò a frequentare nel 1986. Smise il secondo anno perché le lezioni vertevano sull'astrattismo e non erano a lui consone. Così continuò da autodidatta. Una nota su i suoi trompe-l'oeil. Aveva appuntato o bloccato oggetti sulla tela. E di certo gli piaceva, il piegarsi involontariamente per sentire con le dita se la puntina da disegno che teneva l'oggetto ci fosse o non ci fosse. Non c'era. Una delle più notevoli reazioni riguardo l'operato di Frans riguardo l'uso del trompe-l'oeil. Usando le tecniche del chiaroscuro e specialmente del trompe-l'oeil, Frans riesce a catturare togliendo il fiato l'essenza dell'argomento e i pensieri sottintesi. Ma non è un artista a cui piace il legarsi ad un particolare tipo di lavoro sebbene il suo approccio contiene sempre un aspetto di realismo. Qualsiasi sia il percorso scelto il realismo ne farà sempre parte. Frans cerca sempre la terza dimensione sulla superficie piatta, sicché in un articolo di giornale gli viene dato il soprannome di "artista dell'ombra". Le sue opere sono in collezioni private in: Olanda, Belgio, Francia, Inghilterra, America, Irlanda, Curaçao e Svizzera.

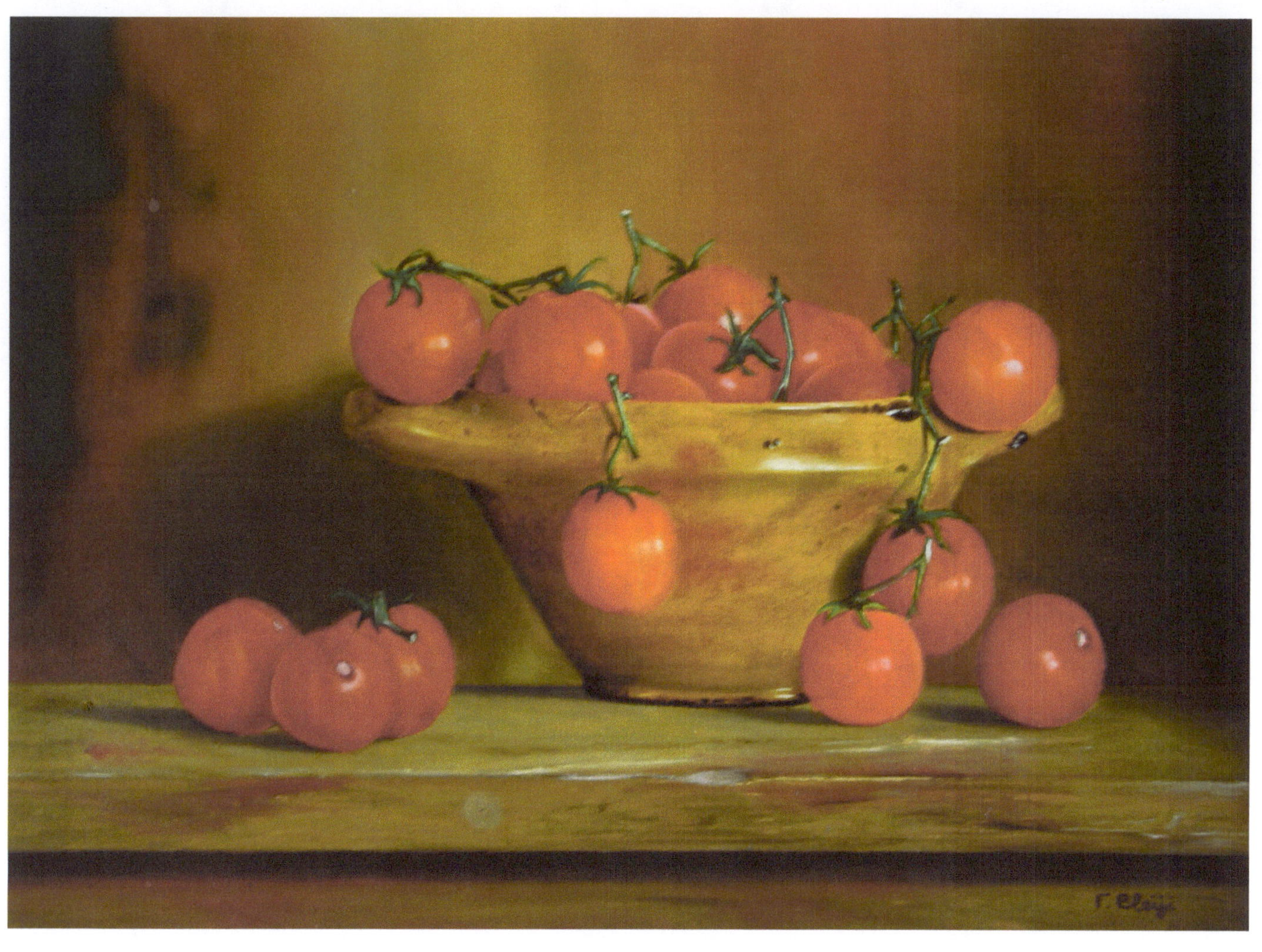

Tomatoes, oil on panel, 23,7x33 cm

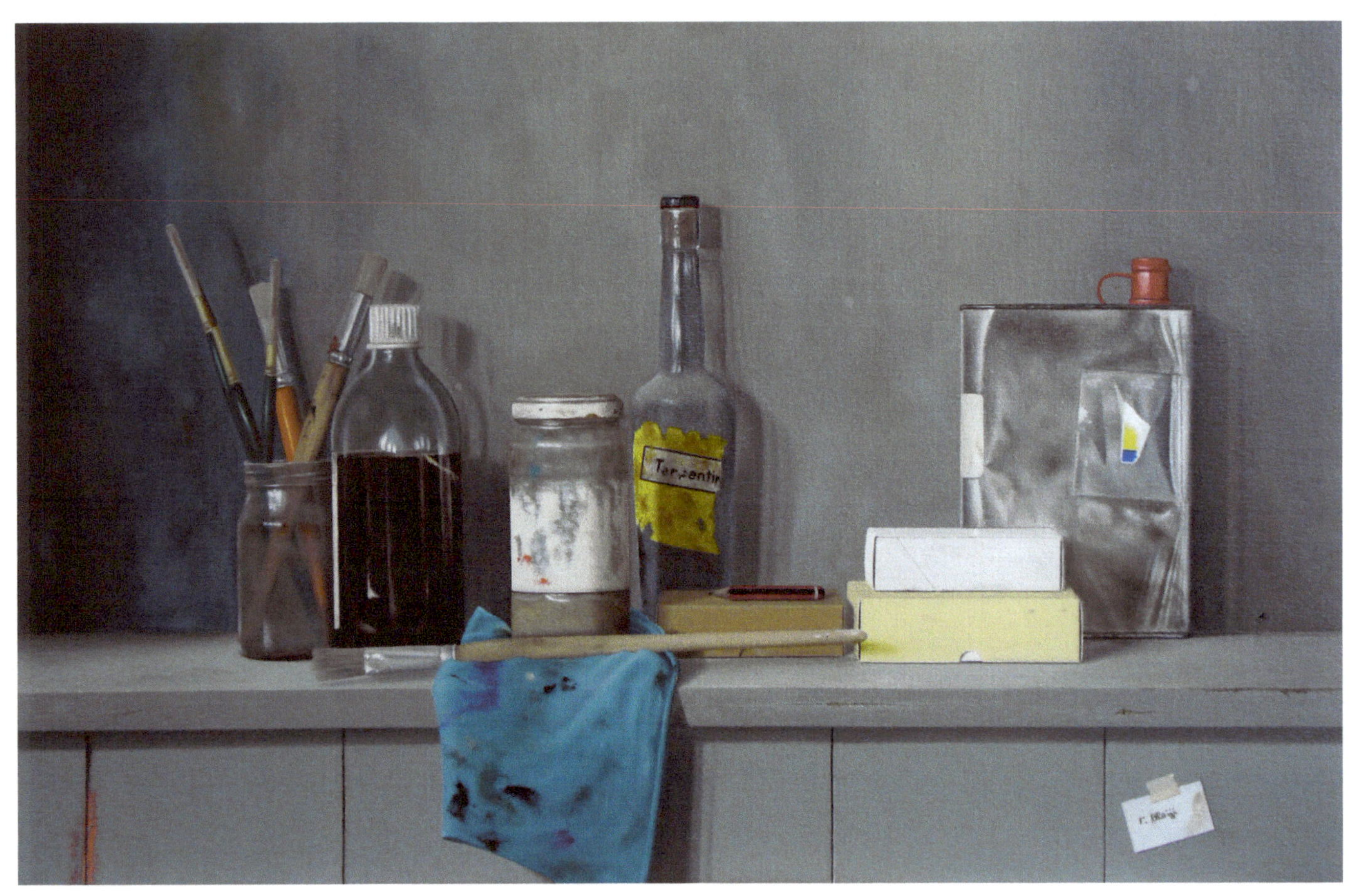

At the studio, oil on linen, 50x80 cm

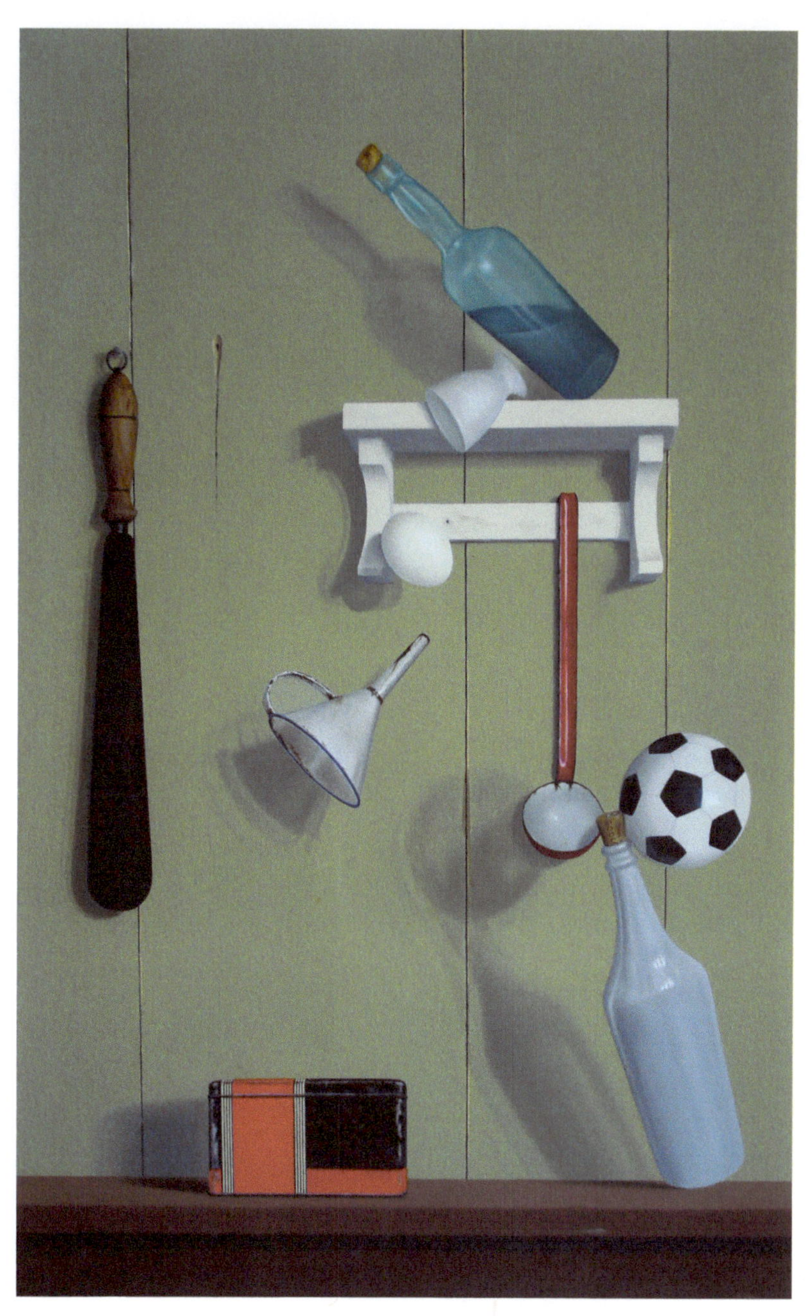

Damage by a ball, oil on linen, 95x60 cm

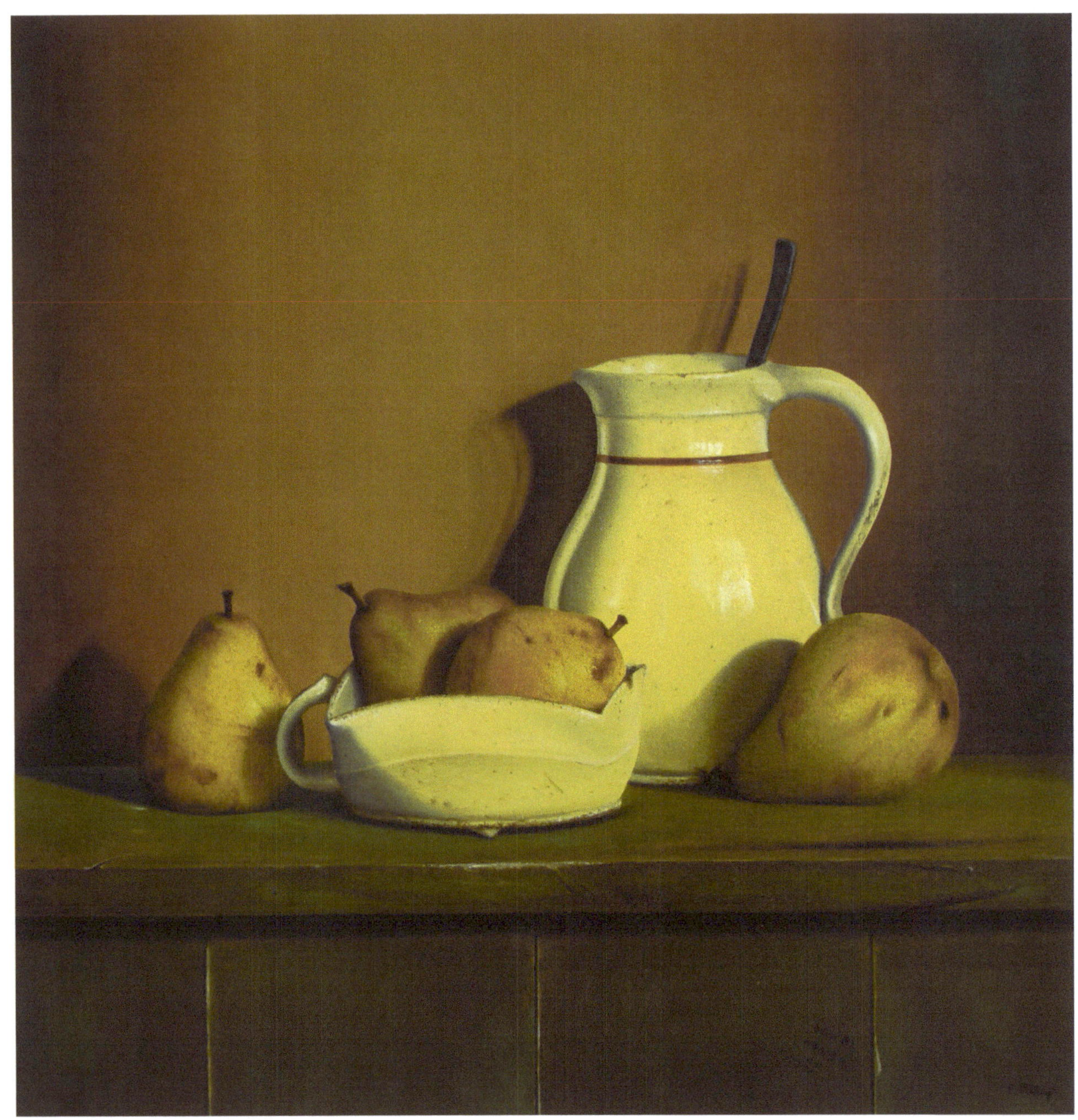

Pears, oil on linen, 50x50 cm

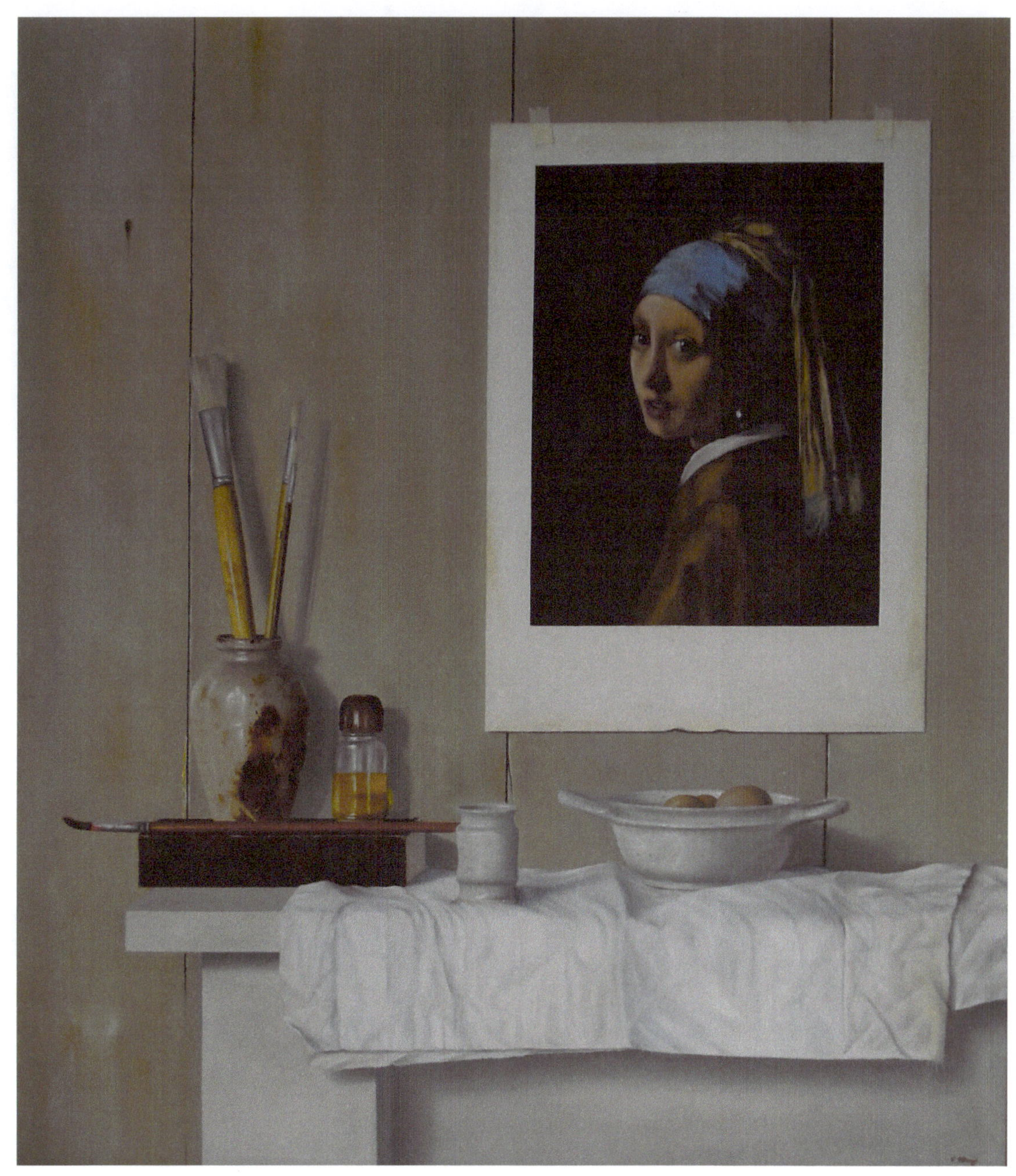

Vermeer's girl, oil on linen, 90x80 cm

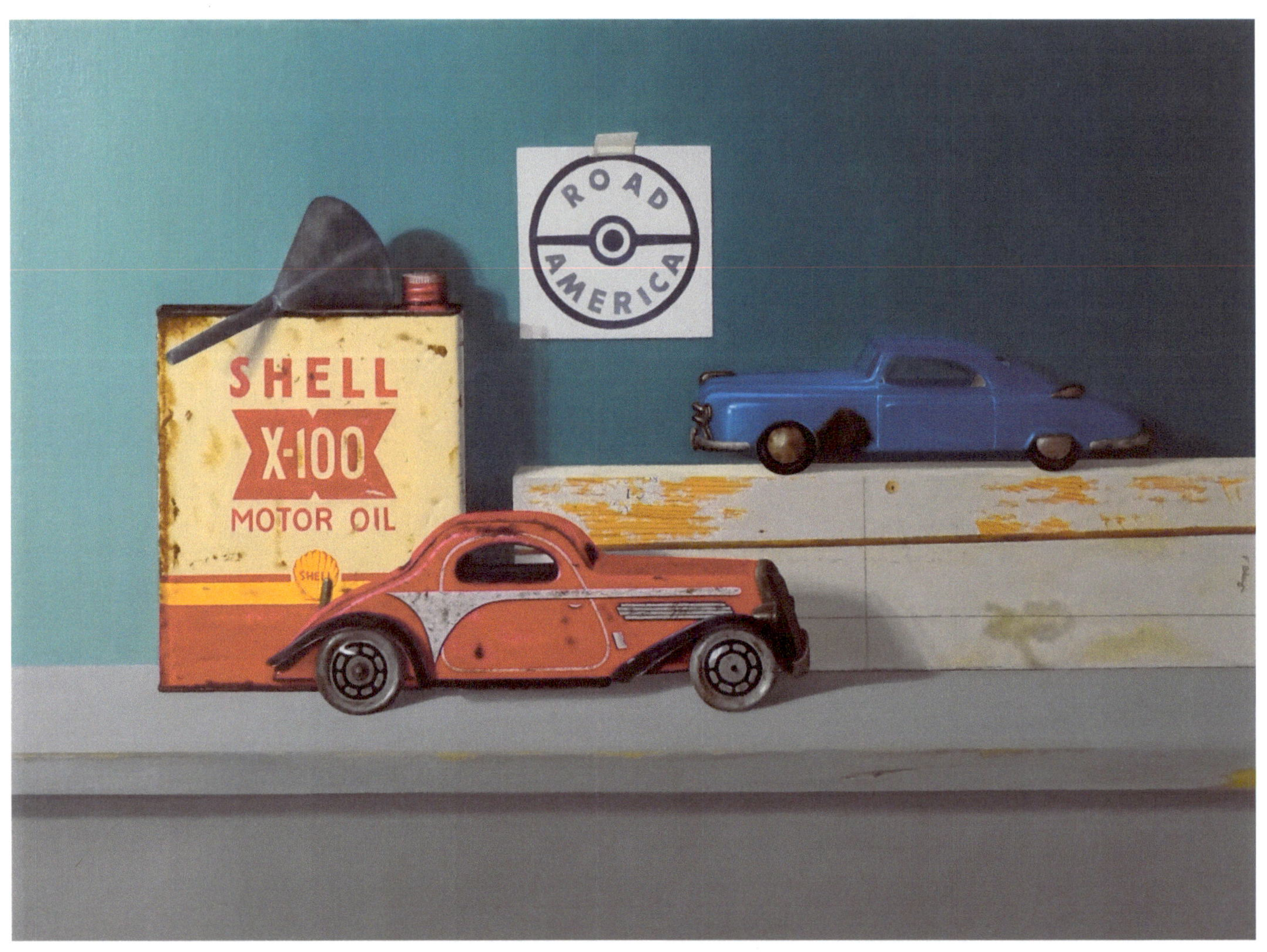

Rusty, oil on linen, 50x70 cm

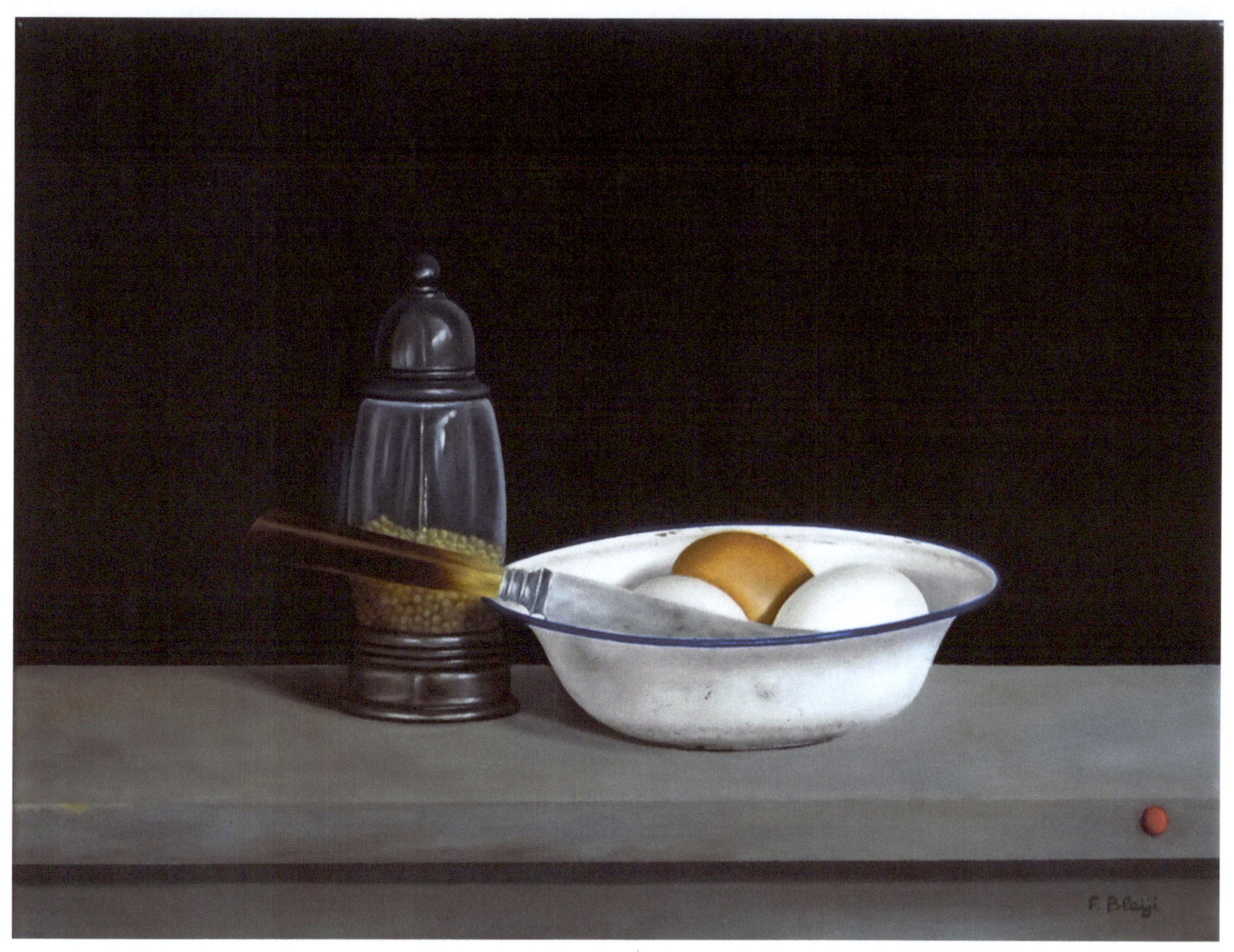

Plate with eggs, oil on linen, 30x40 cm

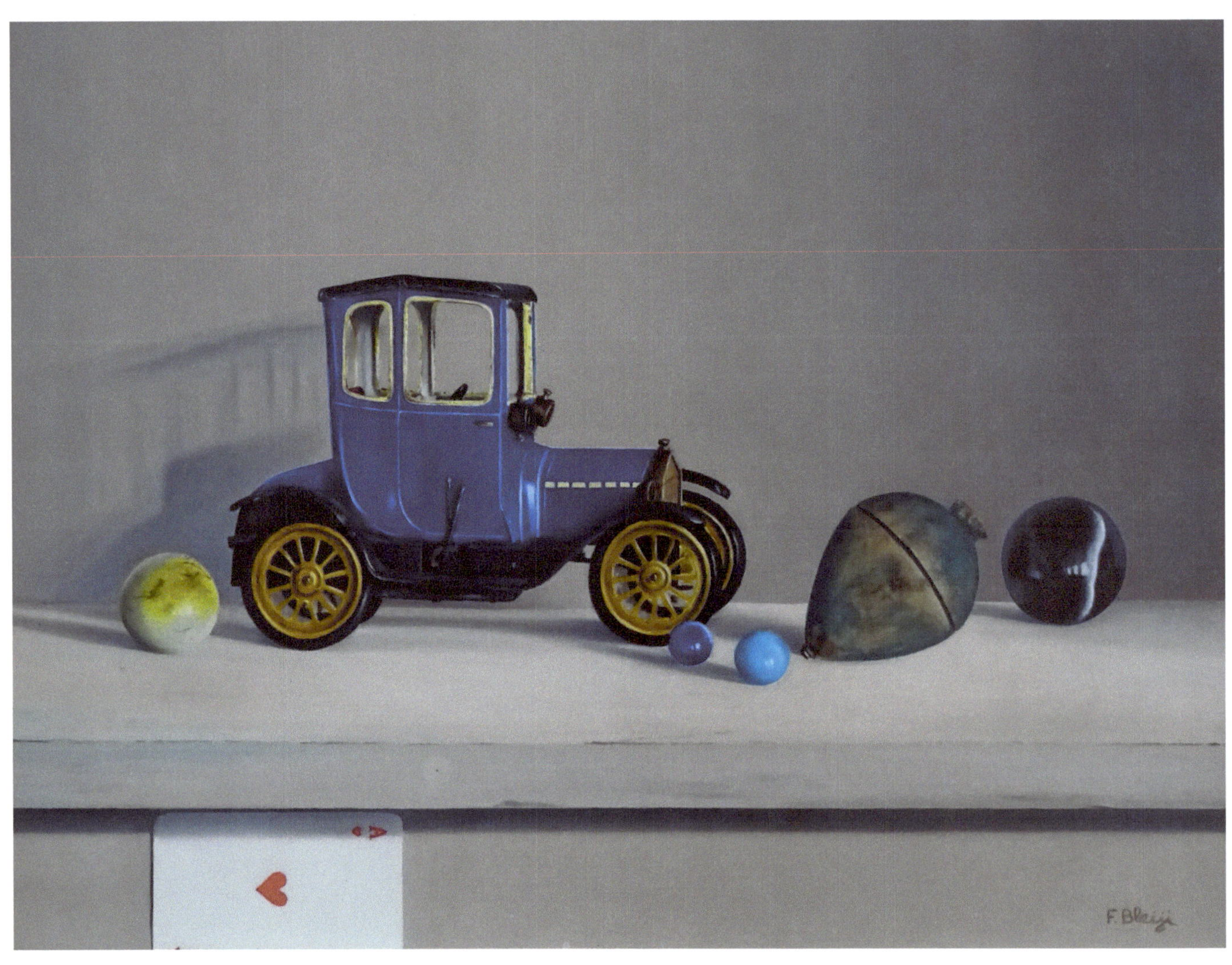

T Ford and marbles, oil on linen, 30x40 cm

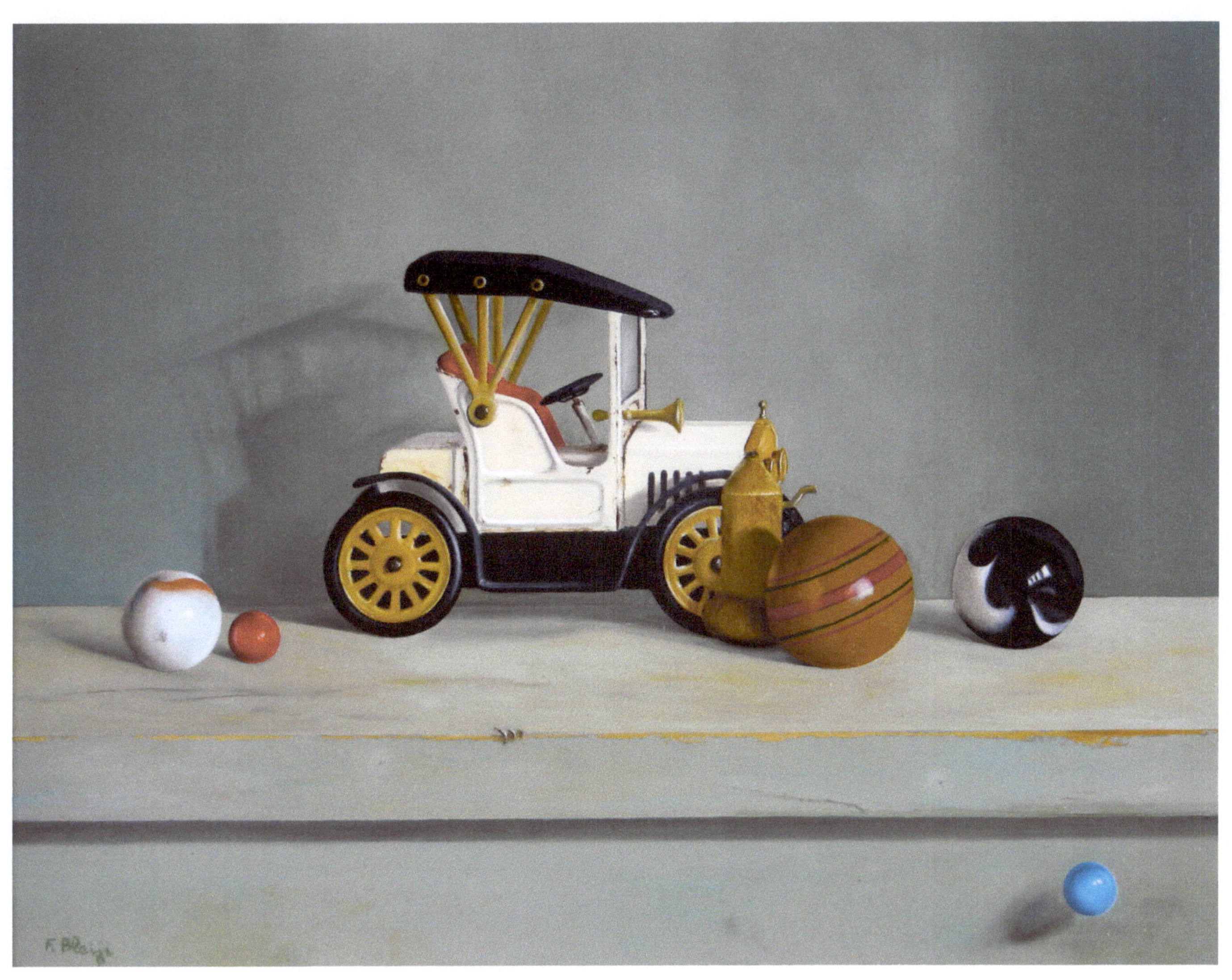

T Ford with marbles 2, oil on panel, 30x40 cm

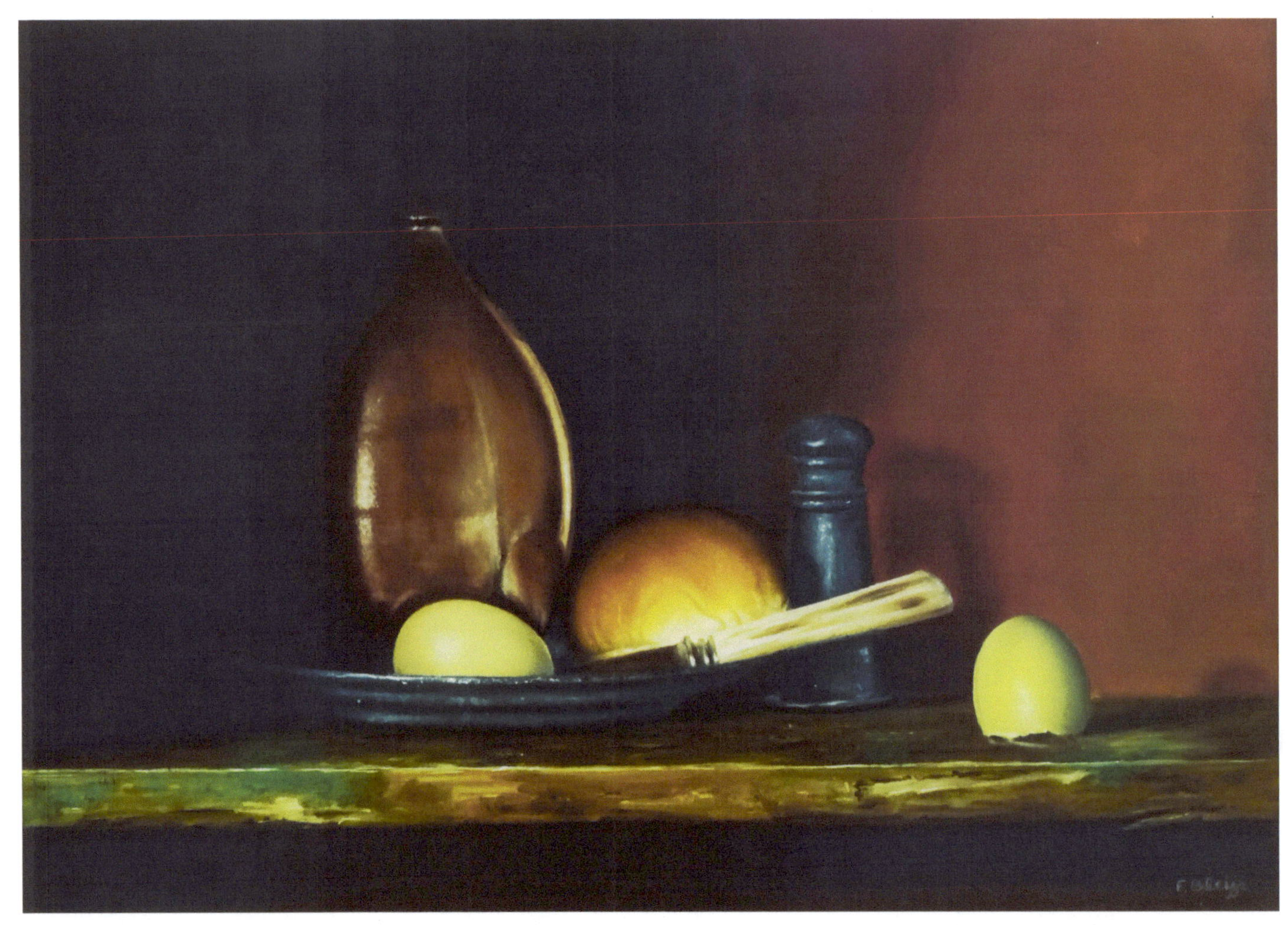

Breakfast, oil on panel, 36x51 cm

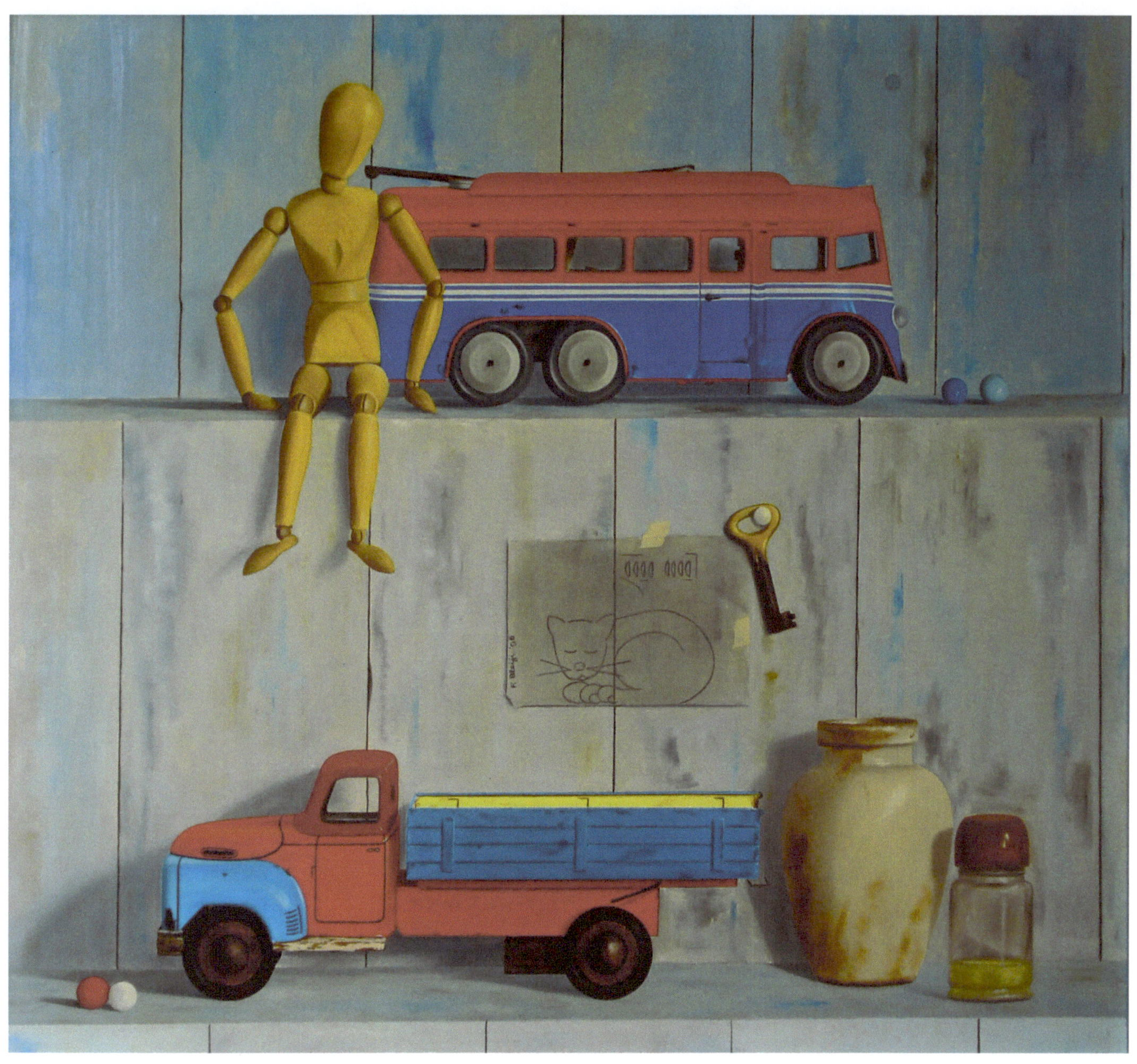

Still life with Toys, oil on panel, 55x61 cm

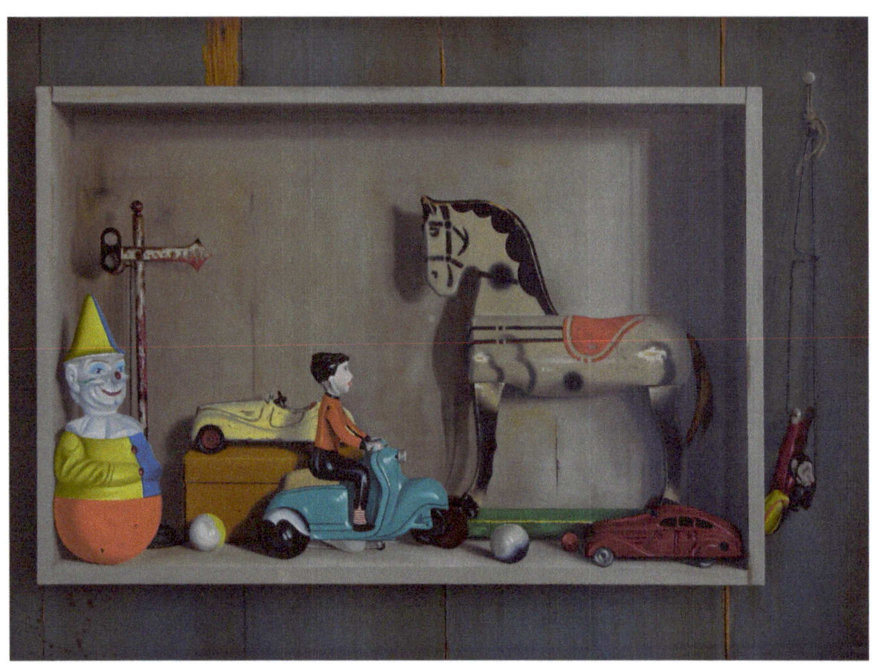

Cabinet with Toys, oil on panel, 55x76 cm

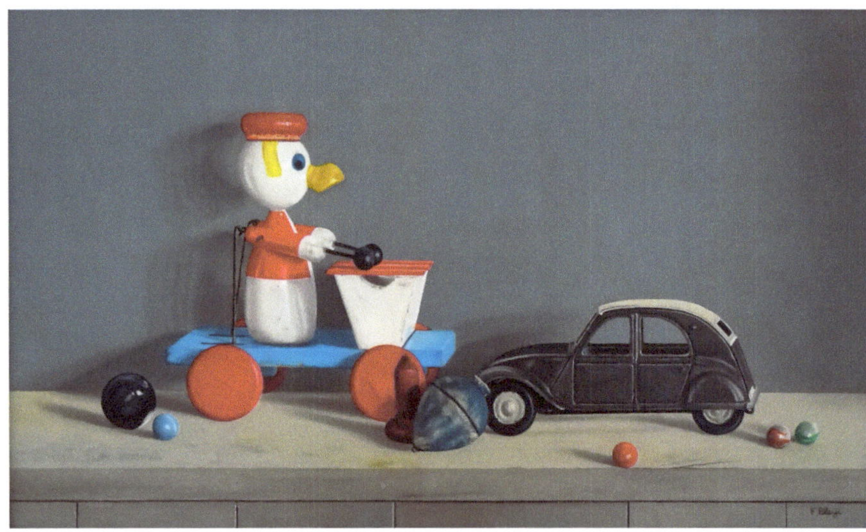

Ugly Duck, oil on panel, 36x61 cm

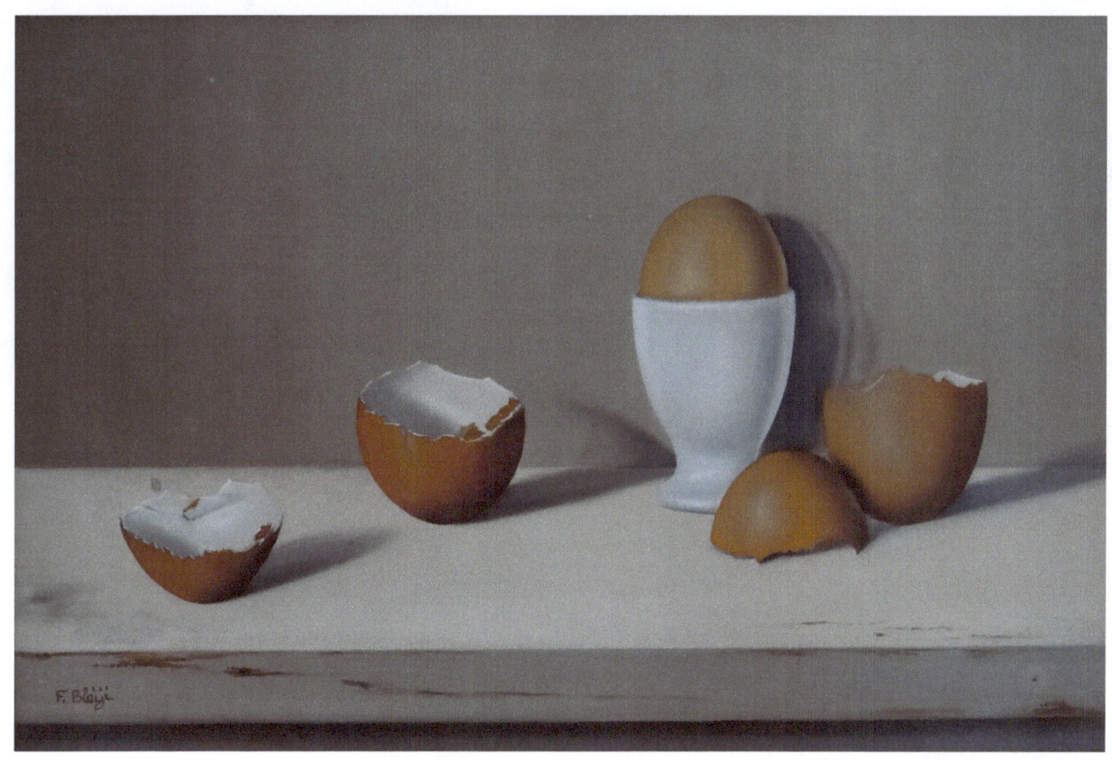

Eggs, oil on panel, 21x32 cm

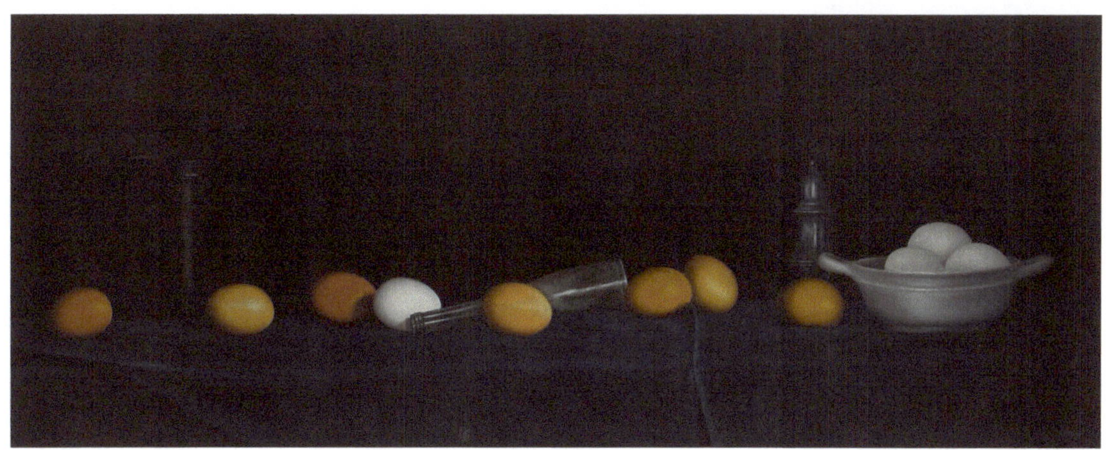

Big meeting, oil on panel, 40x100 cm

13

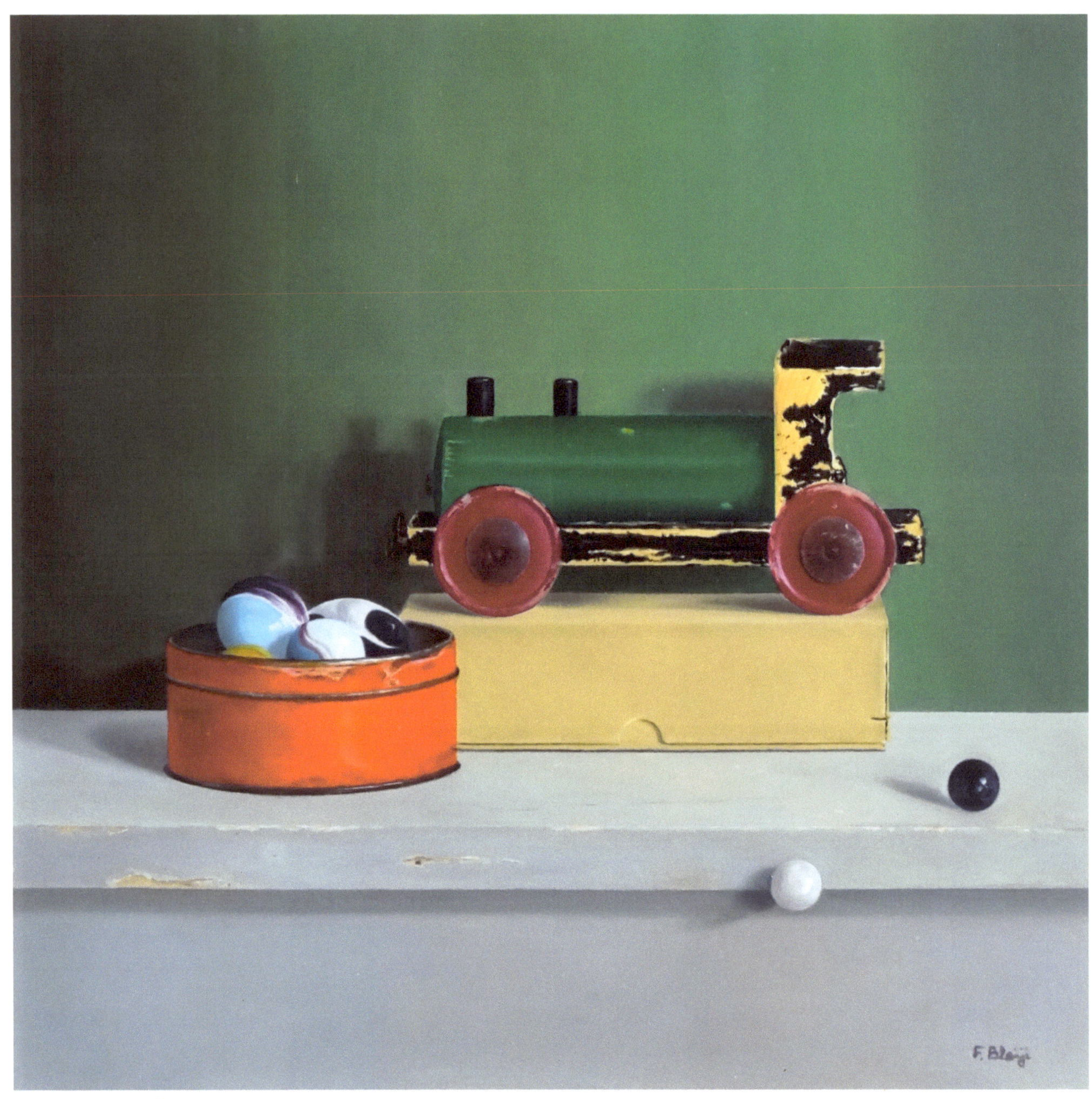

Tin can with marbles, oil on panel, 33x34 cm

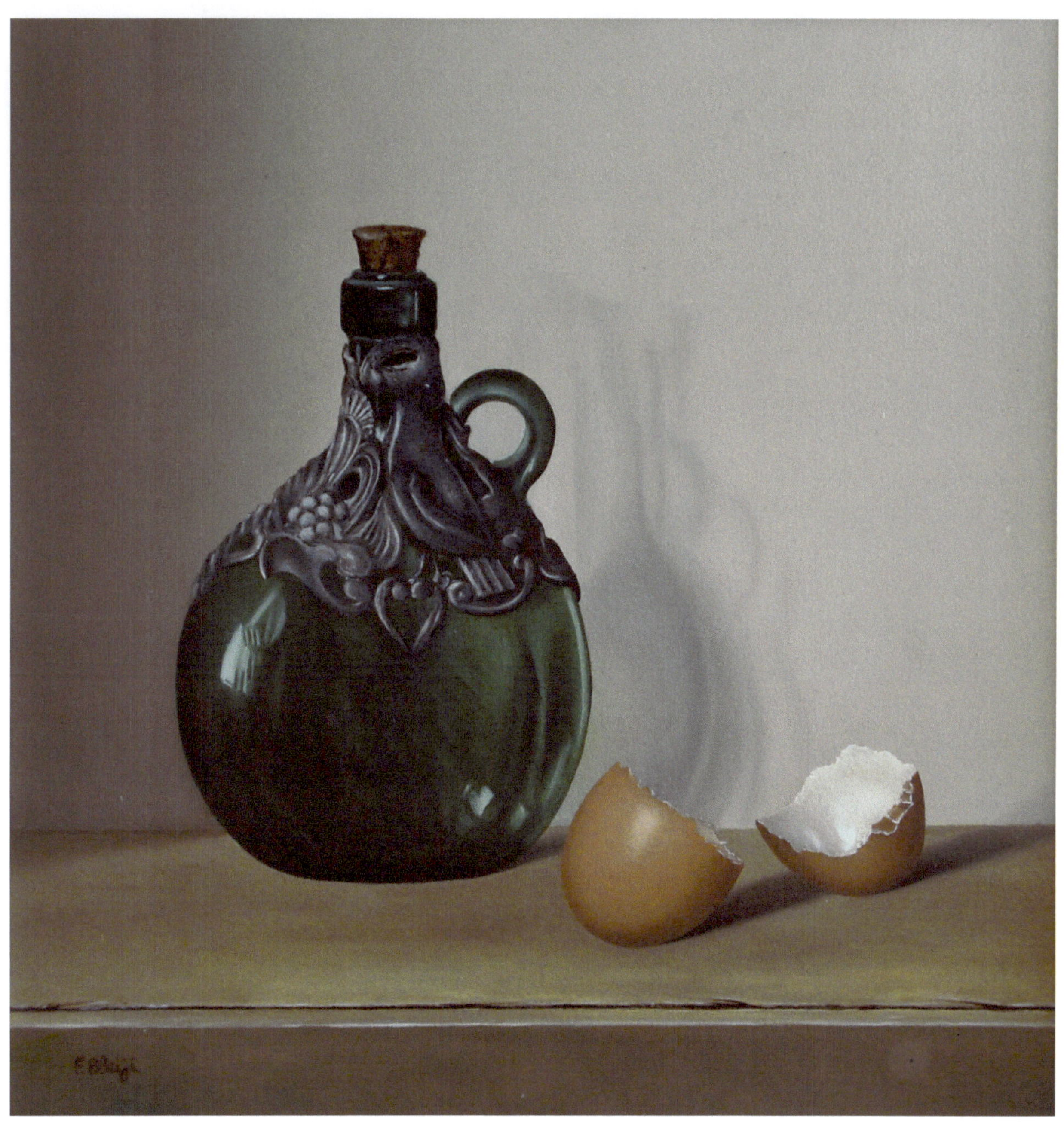

Still life with decanter, oil on panel, 30x30 cm

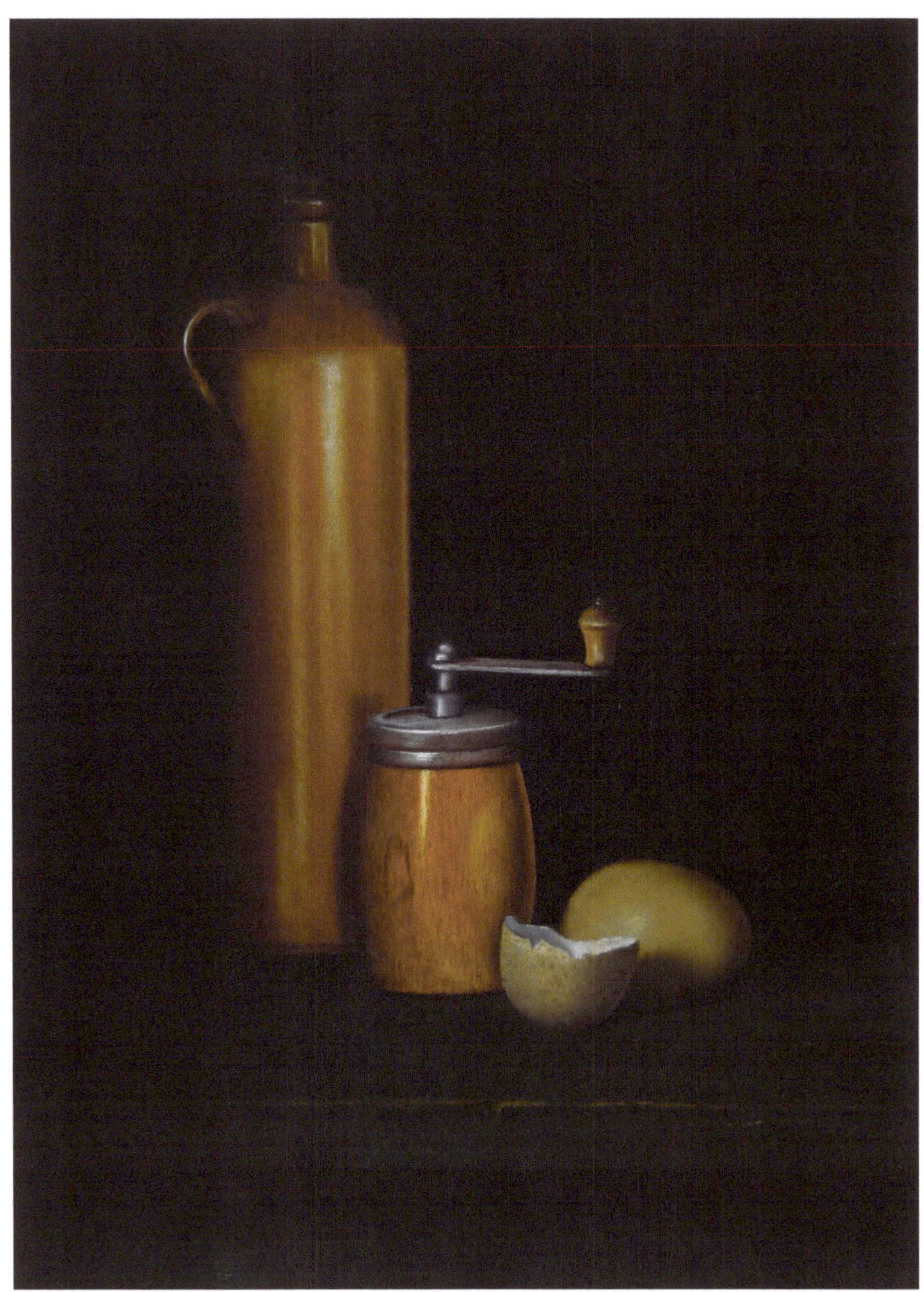

Still life with peppermill, oil on linen, 40x30 cm

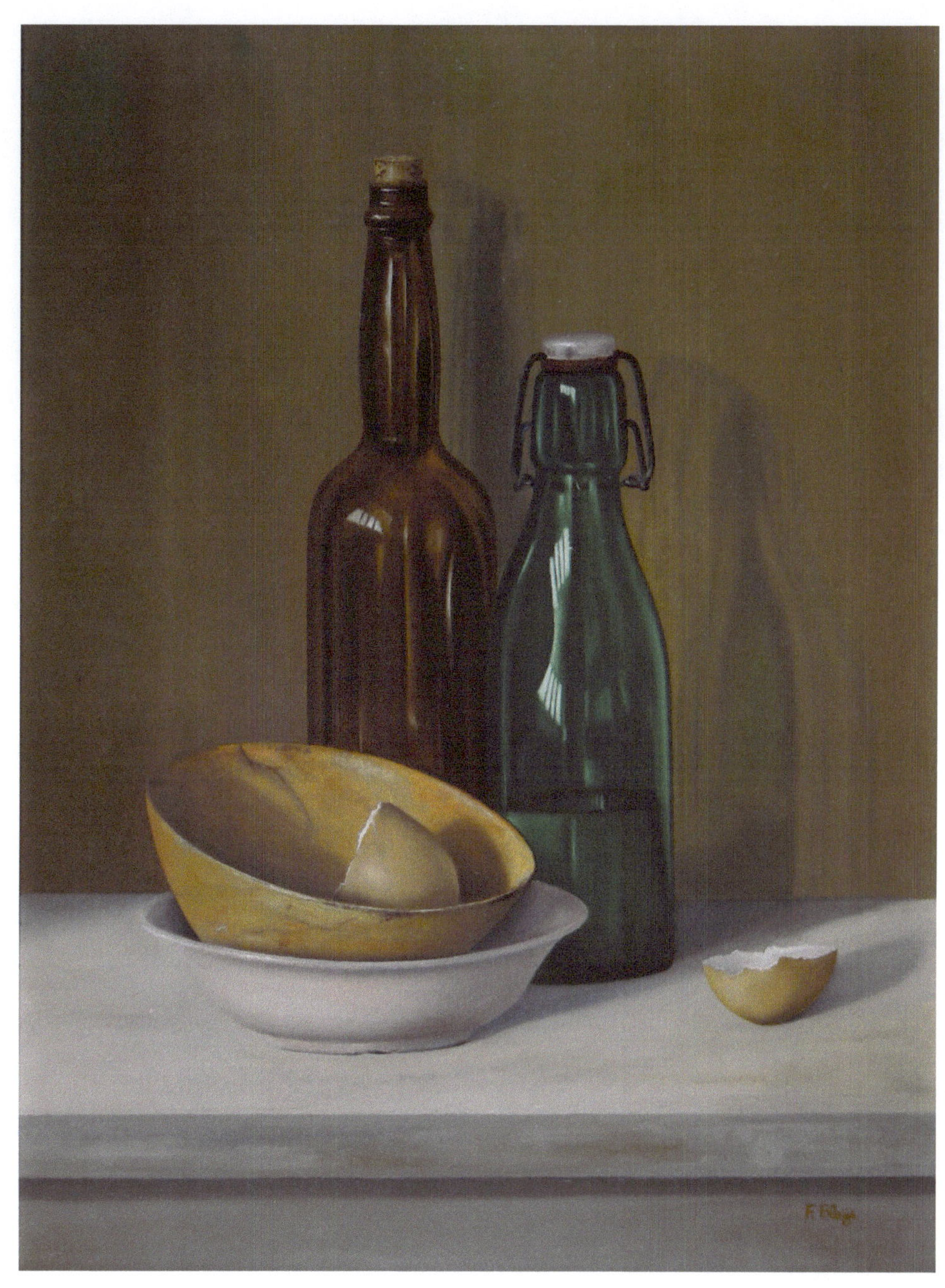

Still life with bottles, oil on panel, 41x31 cm

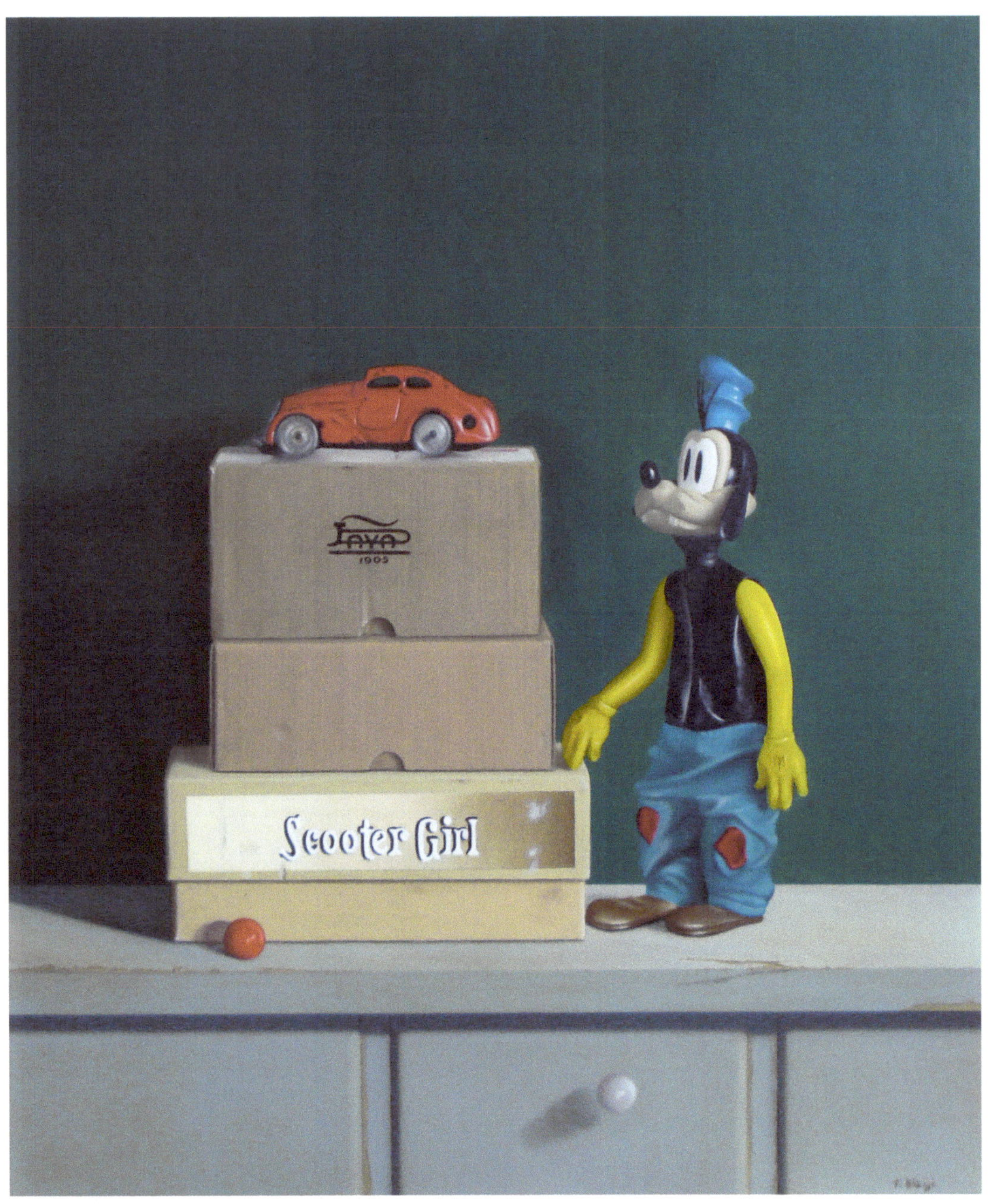

Goofy, oil on panel, 50x42 cm

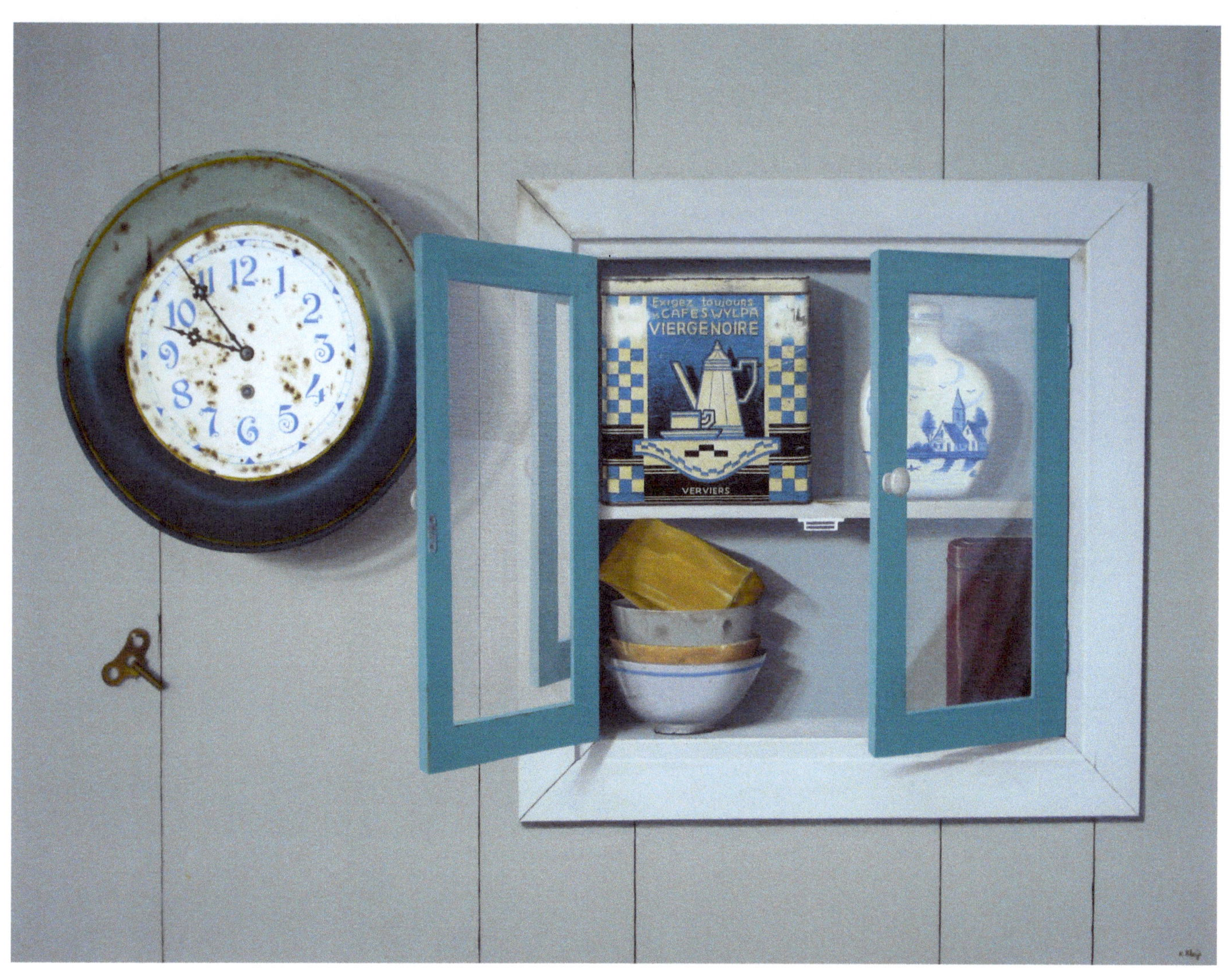

Timeless, oil on linen, 75x100 cm

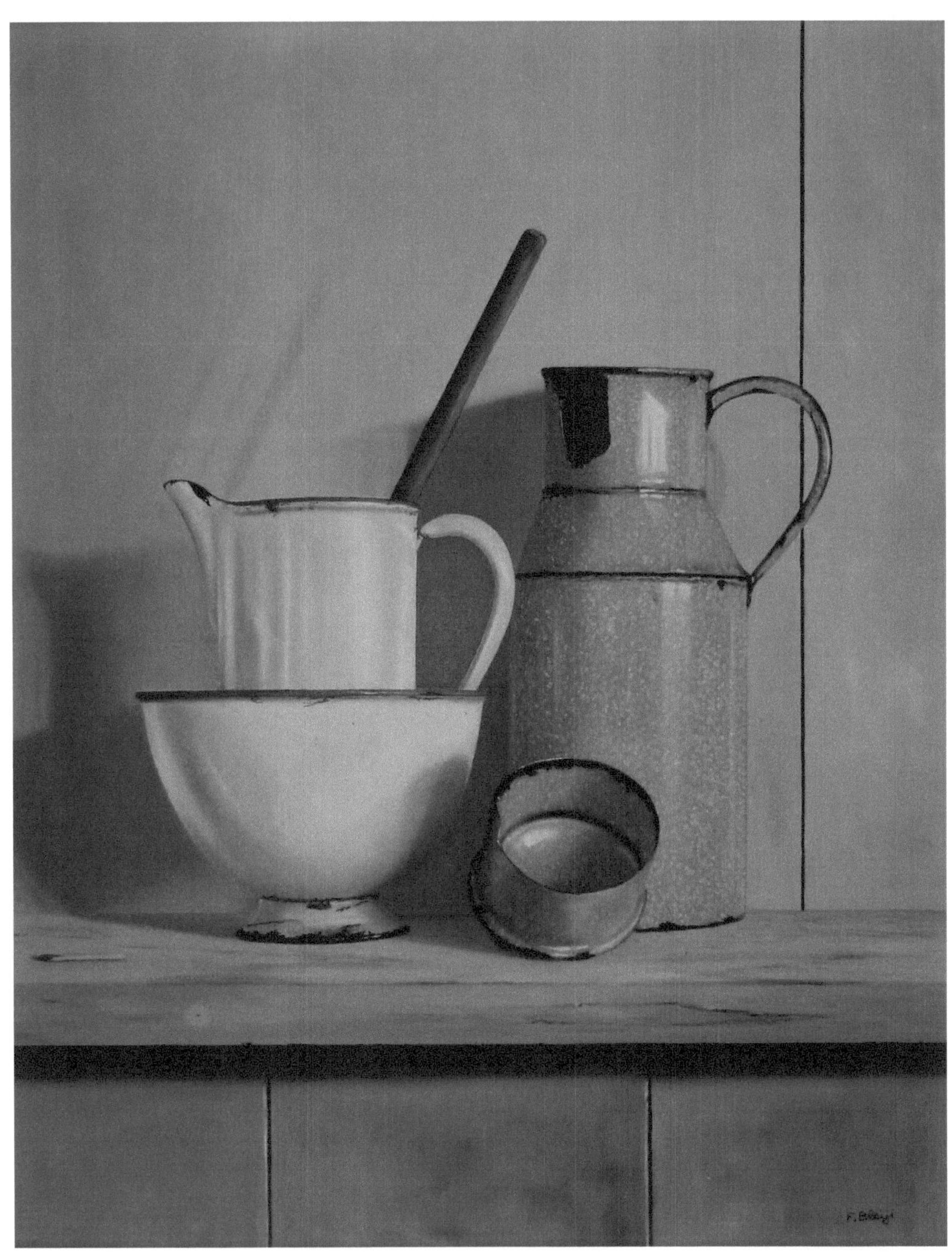

Grey enamel, oil on panel, 50x40 cm

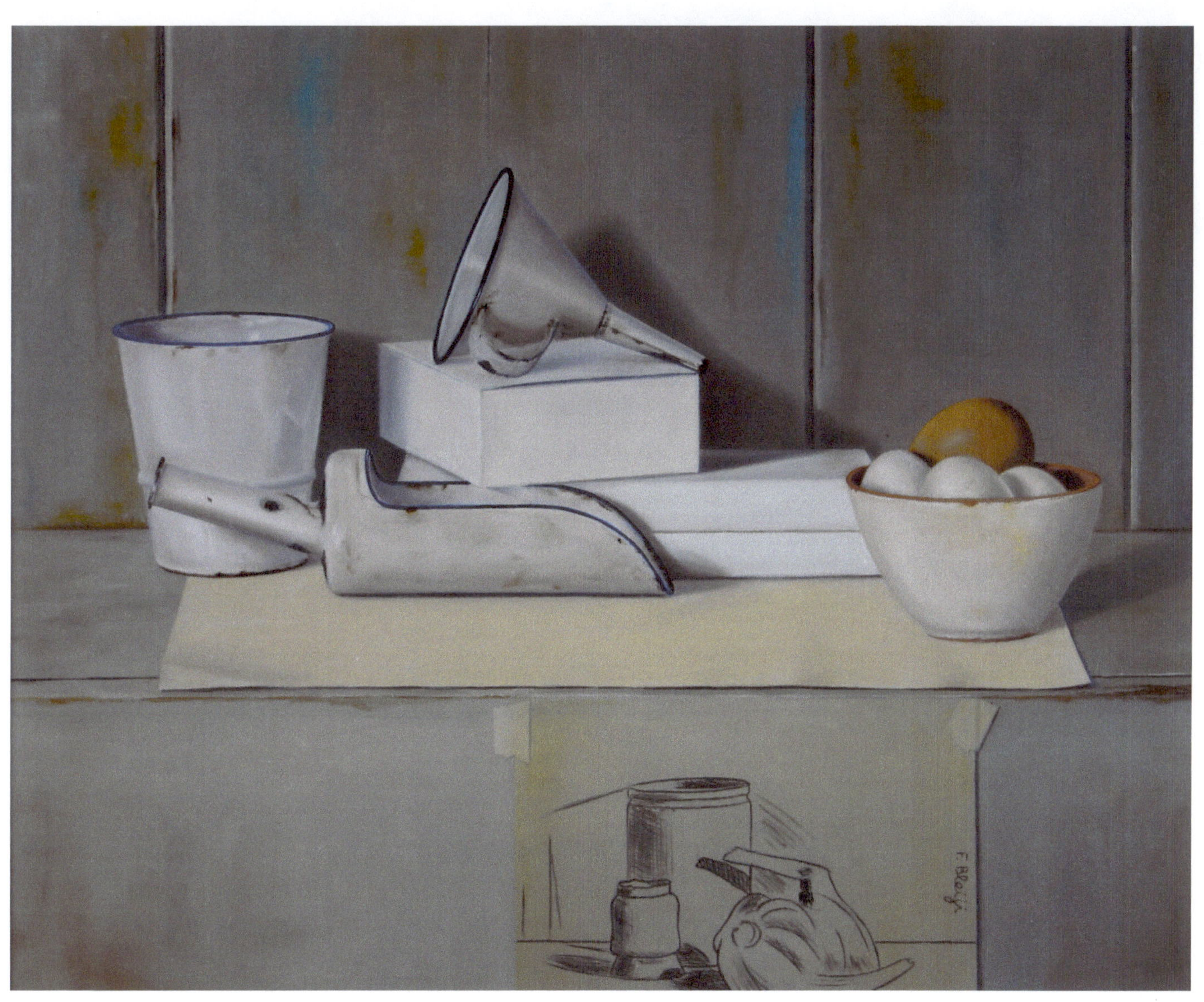

White enamel, oil on panel, 47x57 cm

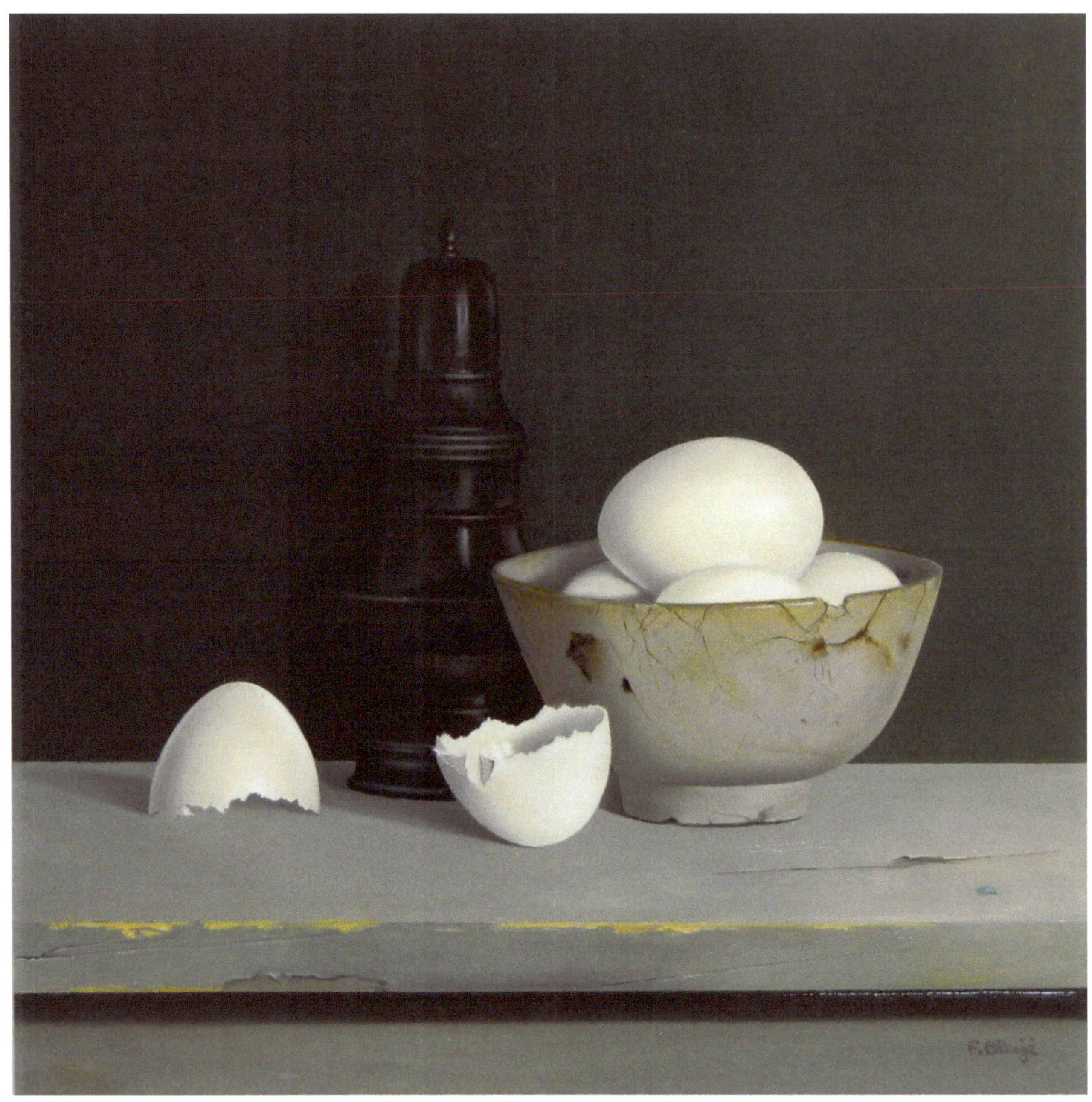

Eggs with salt shaker, oil on panel, 30x30 cm

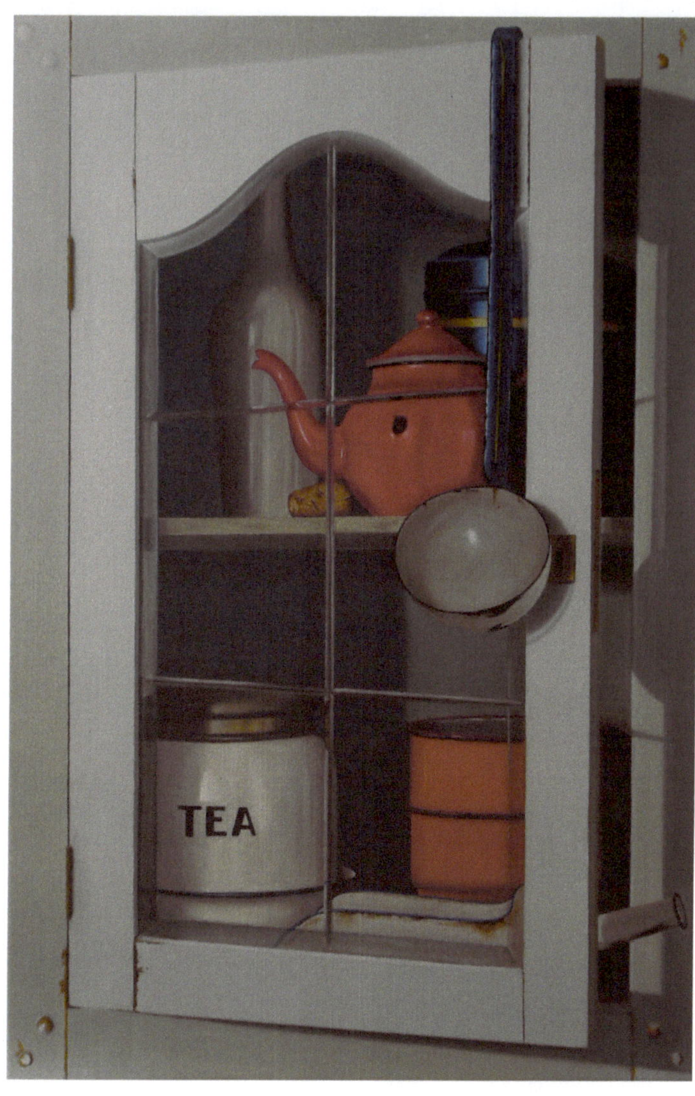

Cabinet with red boiler, oil on linen, 60x40 cm

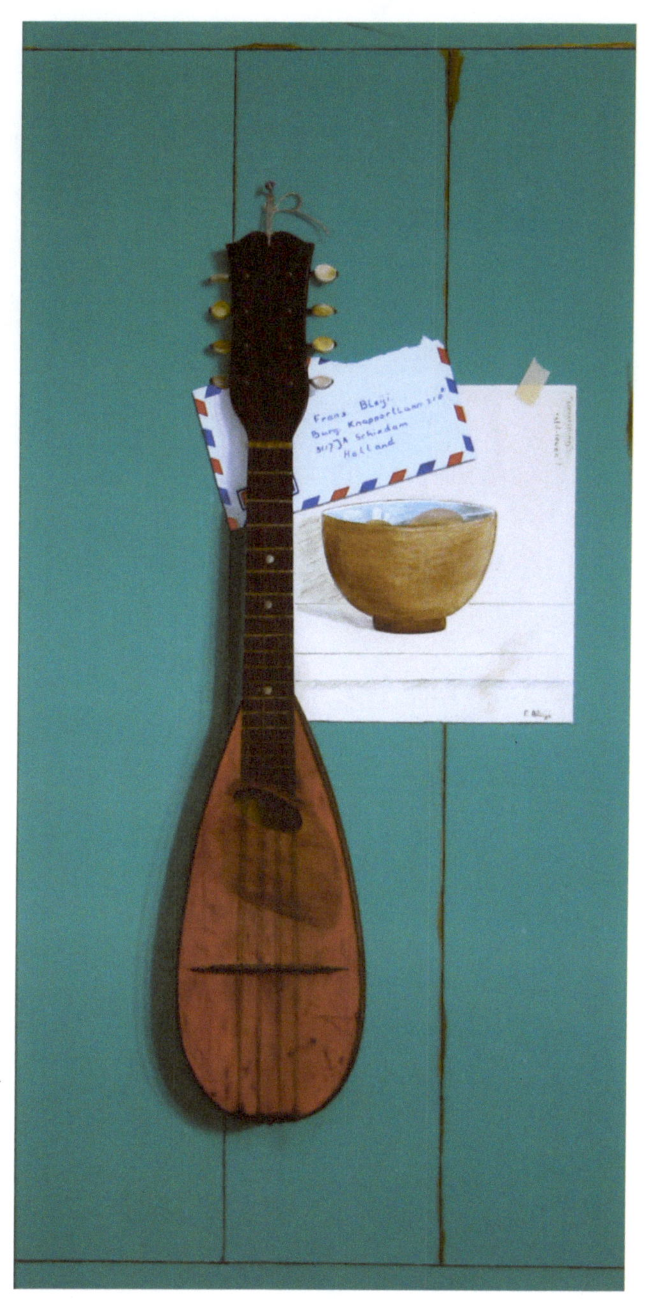

Mandoline, oil on canvas, 40x80 cm

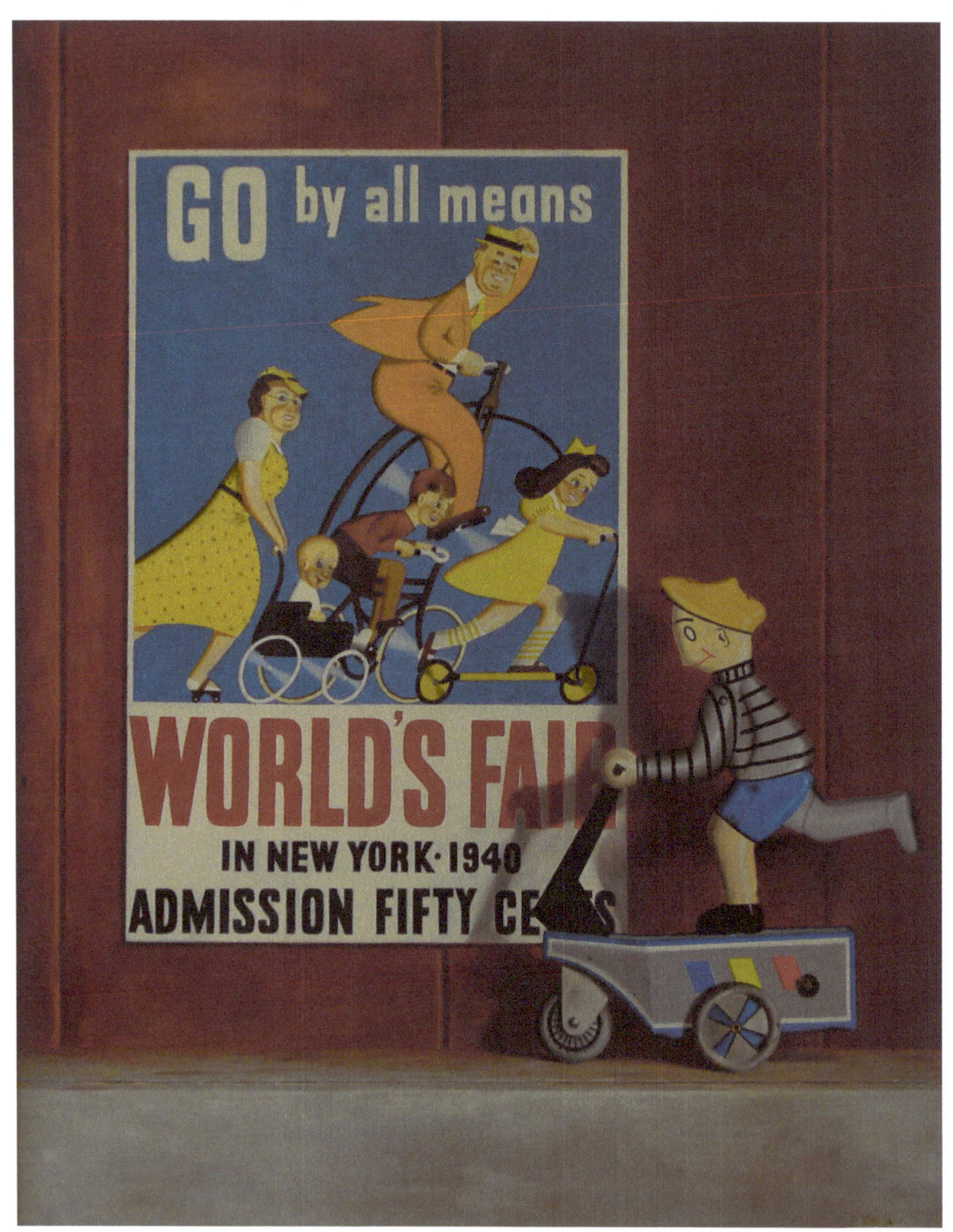

World Fair, oil on canvas, 75x60 cm

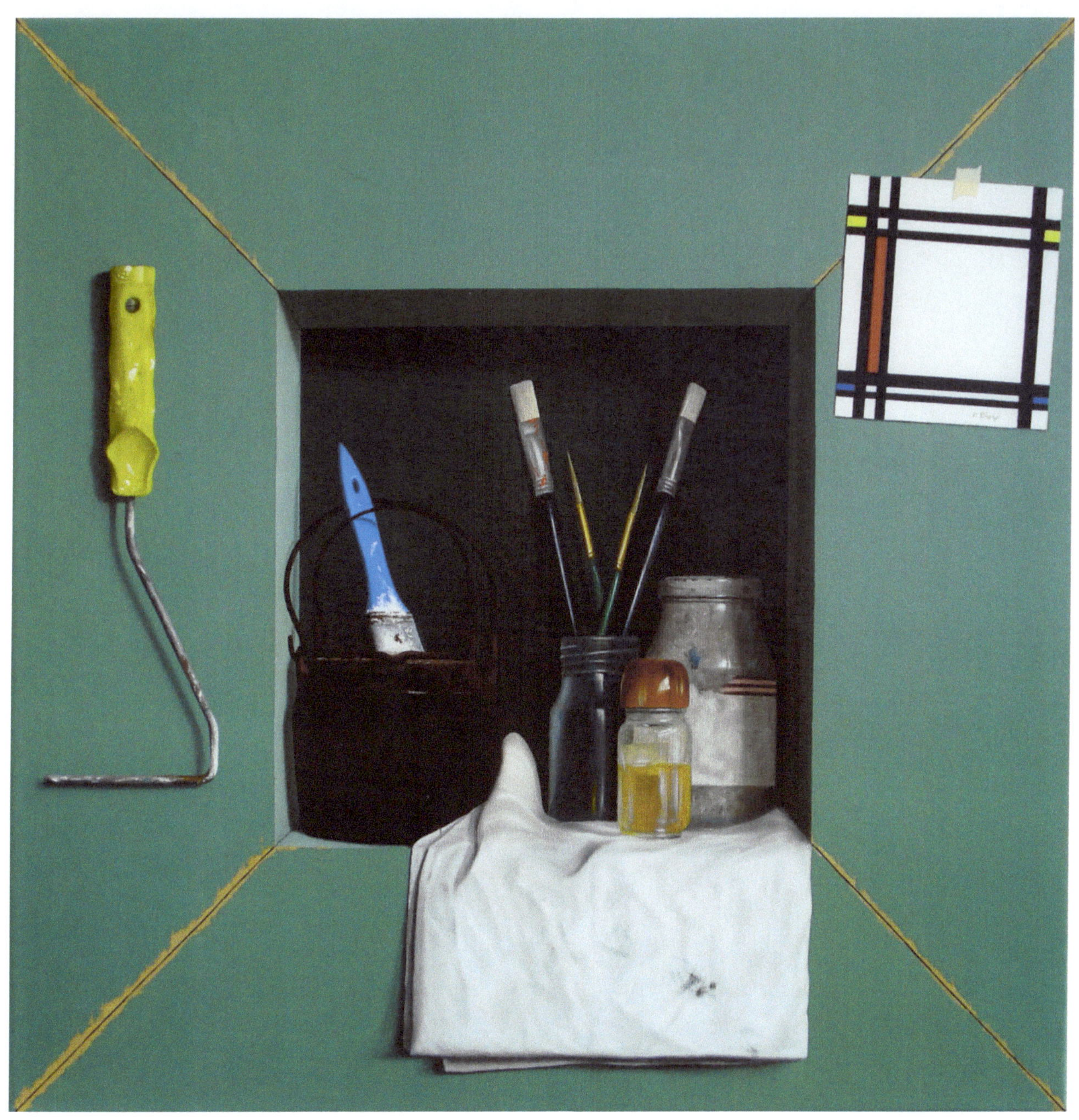

Painters cabinet, oil on linen, 60x60 cm

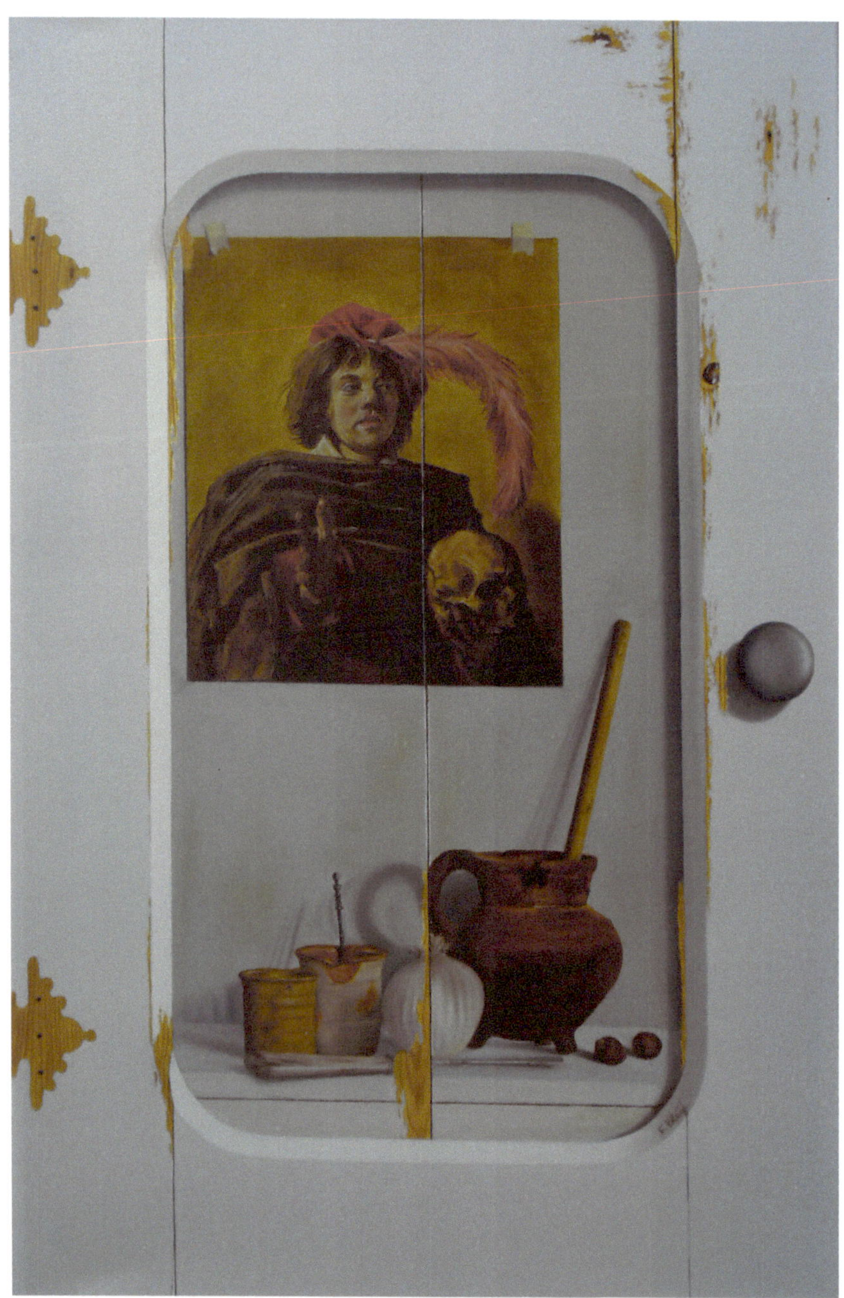

Ode to Frans, oil on canvas, 90x60 cm

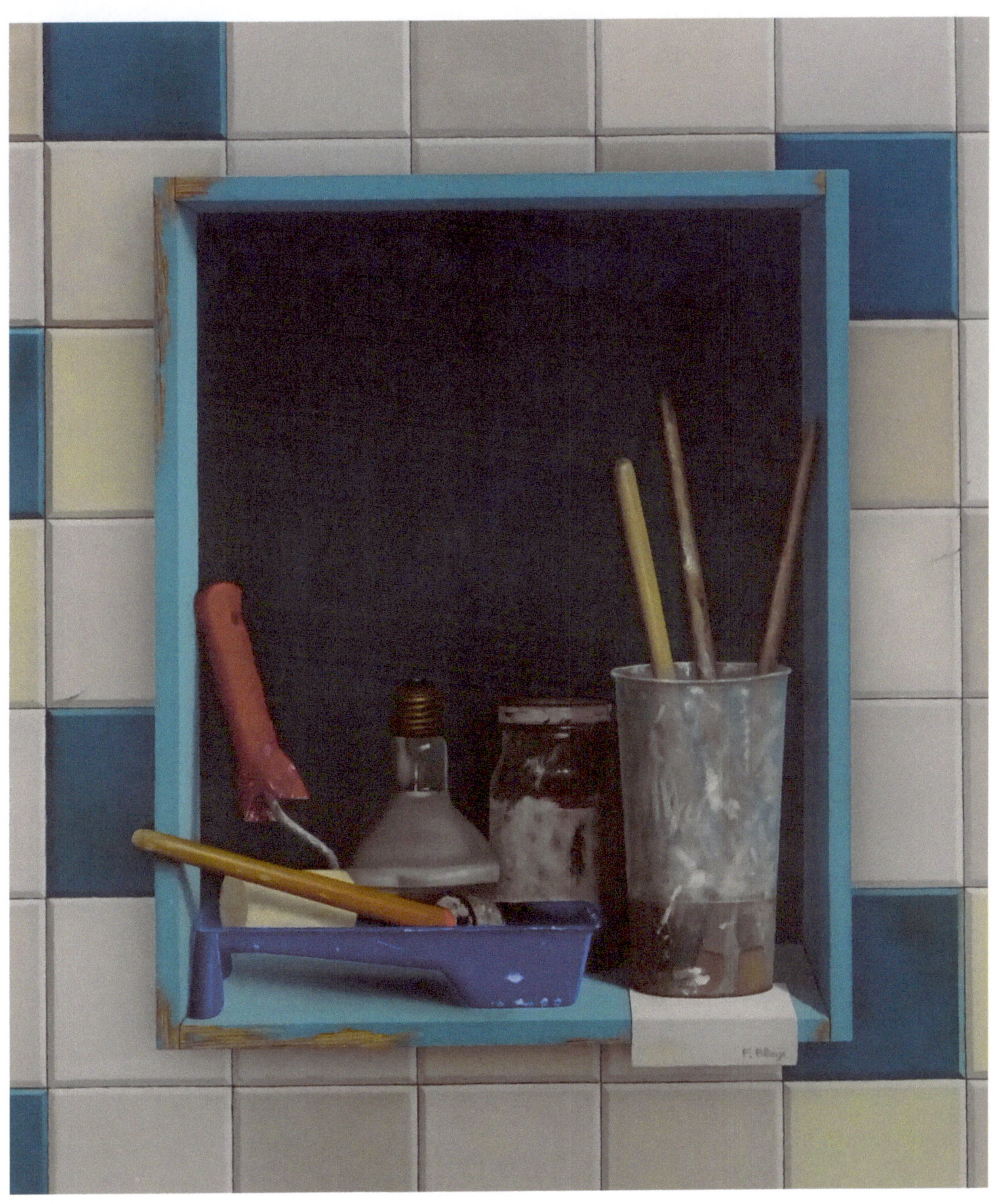

After hard working...!!, oil on panel, 60x52 cm

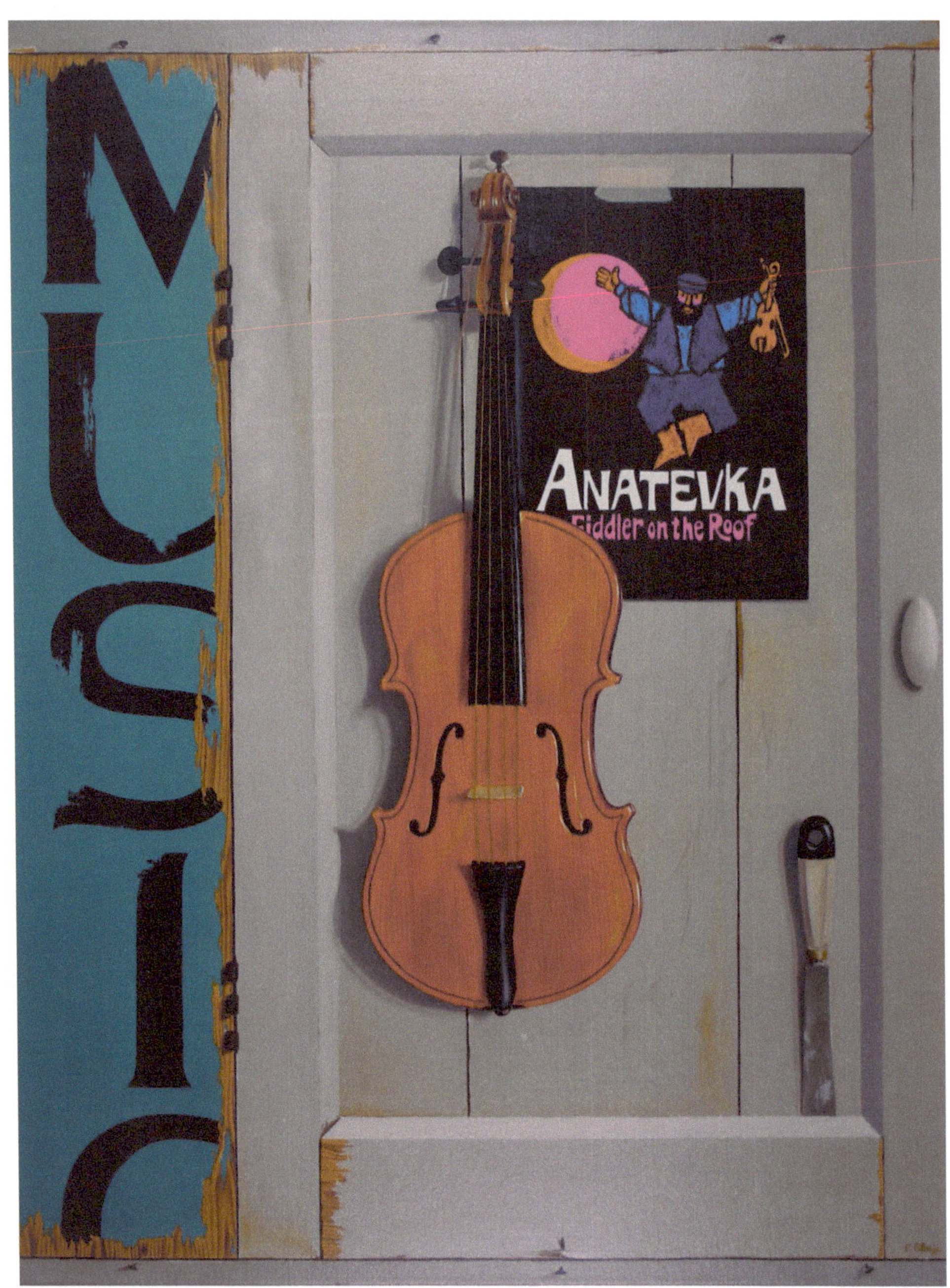

Anatevka, oil on canvas, 90x70 cm

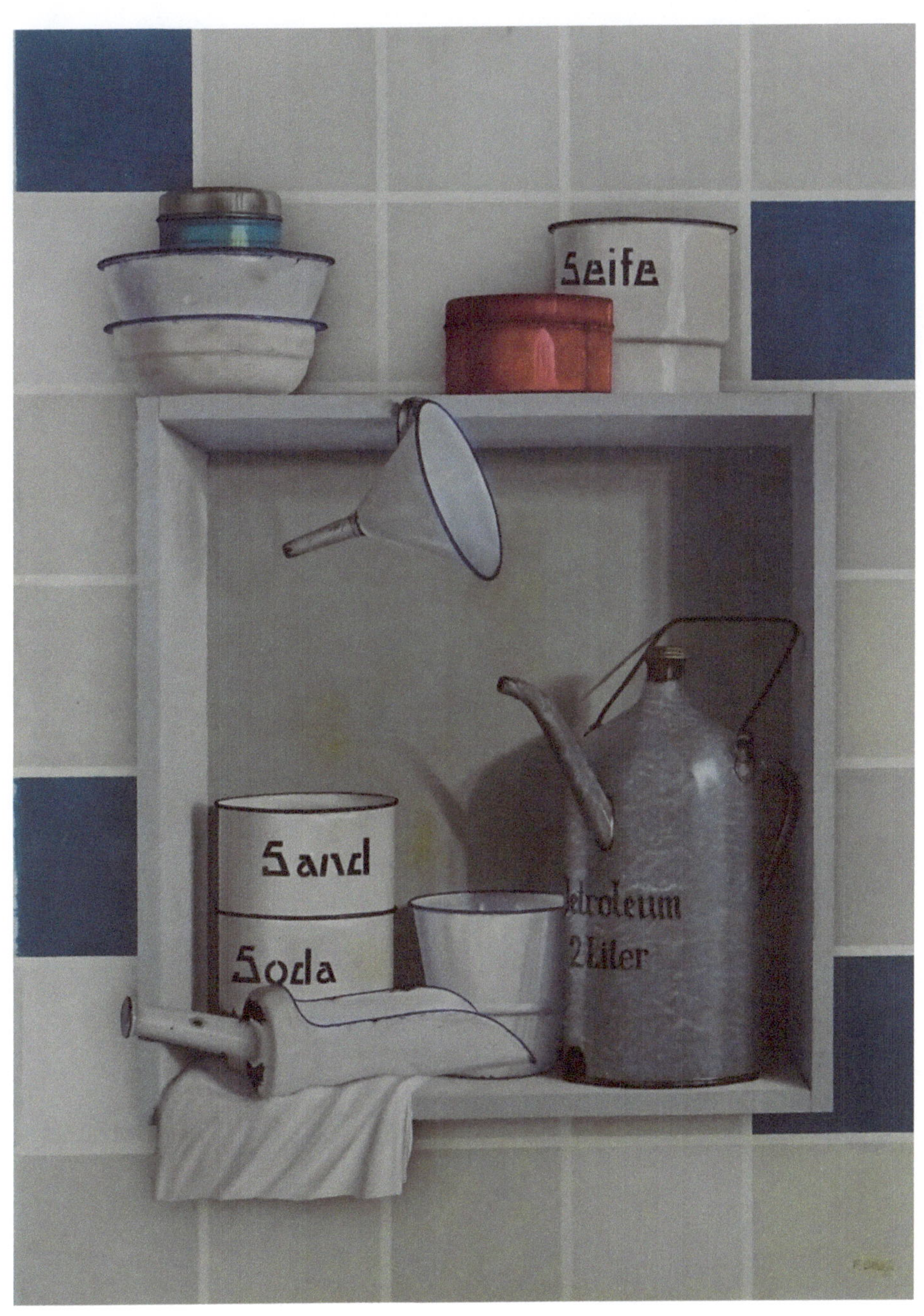

Collected enamel, oil on panel 70x52 cm

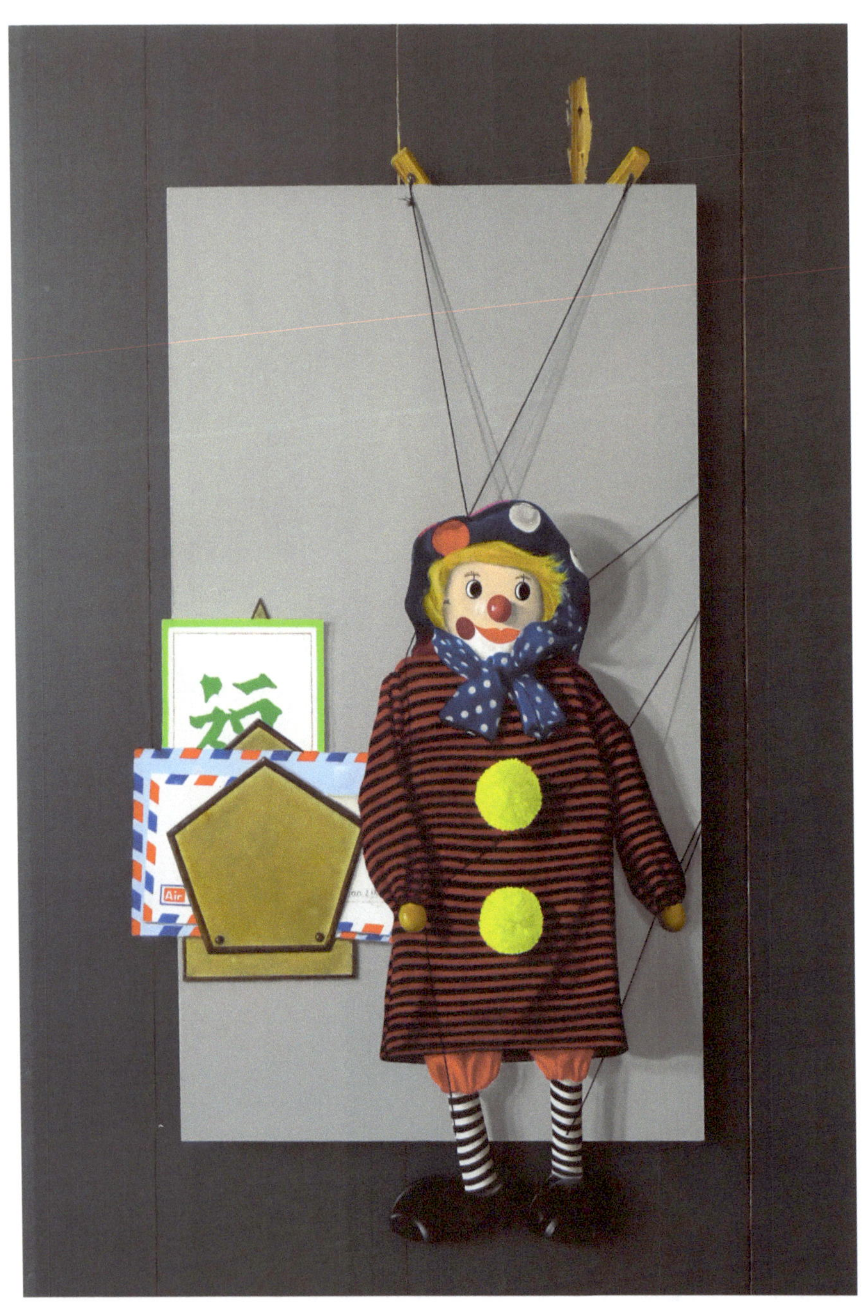

Puppet on a string, oil on panel, 72x52 cm

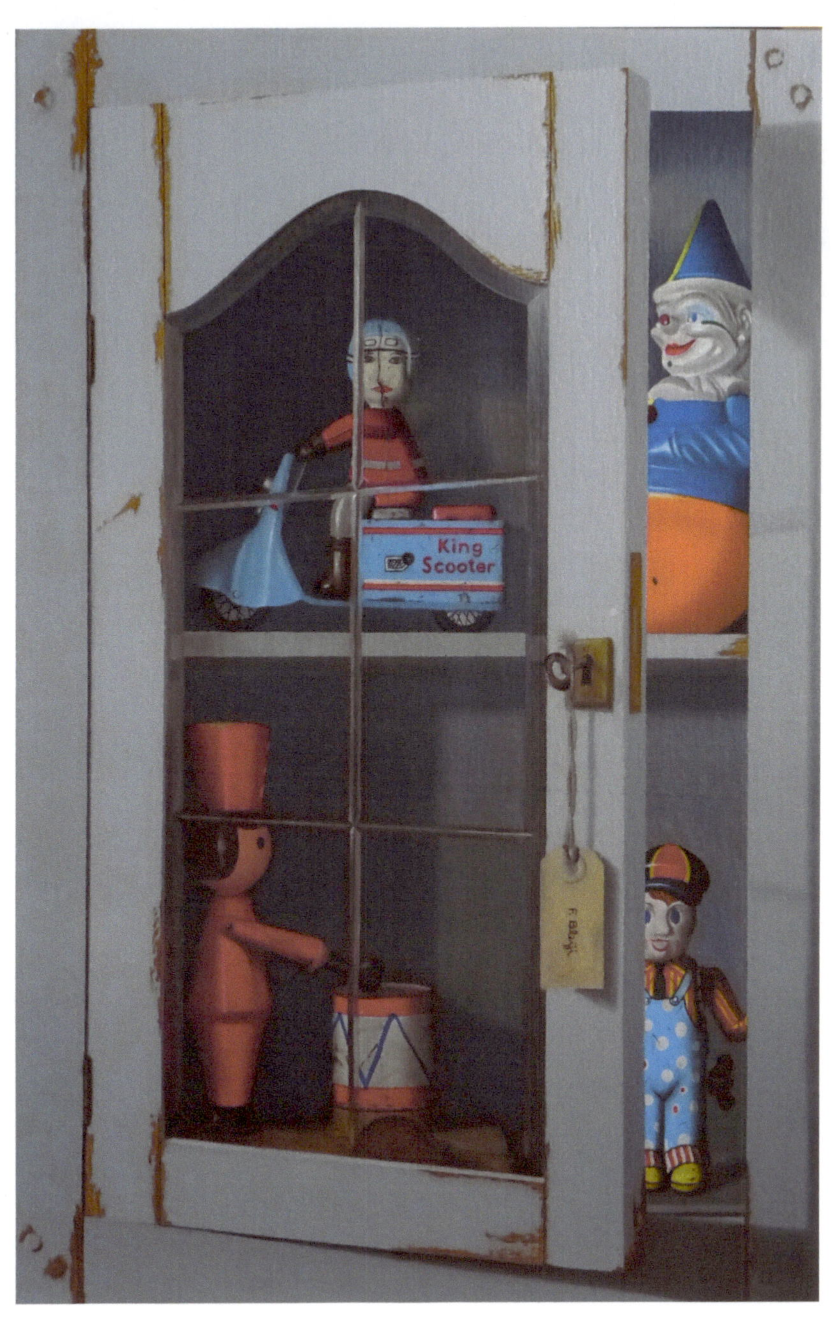

King scooter, oil on linen, 60x40 cm

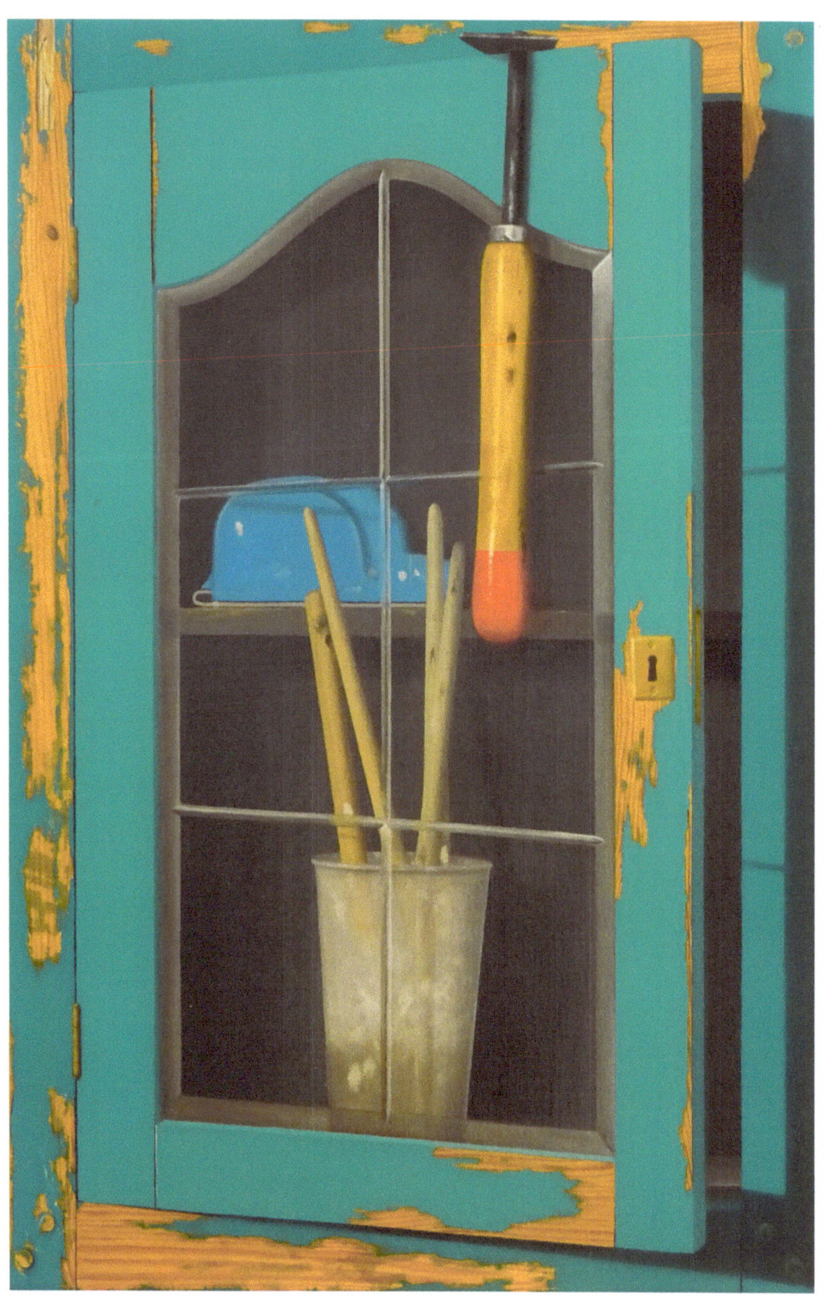

Restoration project, oil on linen, 60x40 cm

Alphabetical index of published pictures

9 788889 427430